The Case of James Harry Reyos

A Wrongful Conviction Revealed

Scott Lomax

An S C Lomax Publication

Copyright © Scott Lomax 2017

Text Copyright © Scott Lomax 2017

The Rights of S C Lomax to be identified as the author of this work have been asserted in accordance with sections 77 and 78 of the Copyright Designs and Patents Act 1988.

All rights reserved. No part of this publication may be reproduced, stored in a retrieval system, or transmitted in any form or by any means, electronic, mechanical, photocopy, recording or otherwise, without prior written permission of the copyright owner. Nor can it be circulated in any form of binding or cover other than that in which it is published and without similar condition including this condition being imposed on a subsequent purchaser.

Preface

'On June 10, 1983, I was wrongly convicted of the murder of Father Patrick Ryan, a Catholic priest. I spent 22 years in prison for this crime – while the REAL KILLER roamed free, and who is still free today. There is substantial and powerful evidence PROVING my innocence. Even the former prosecuting attorney now believes that he convicted an innocent man. There exists powerful evidence PROVING my innocence. The bottom line is I DID NOT KILL FATHER PATRICK RYAN! I AM TRULLY INNOCENT!!! My case is currently being reviewed by the Texas Board of Pardons and Paroles, which will eventually make a final recommendation to Governor Rick Perry. The ONLY right decision that the Board can make – in the interests of justice! – is to recommend "Full Pardon Based on Innocence." Nothing less will suffice. JUSTICE demands that final decision.'

These are the words of James Harry Reyos, a Native American man jailed in 1983 for murdering Irish born Catholic priest, Father Patrick Ryan.

Sentenced to 38 years in prison, the authorities felt sure that Reyos was the man who brutally murdered Father Ryan shortly before Christmas in 1981. They were equally sure he was guilty when Reyos attempted to appeal against his conviction. It was only after Reyos lost his appeal that the prosecuting attorney realized he had got it wrong, but by then it was too late, leaving Reyos frequently asking 'Why am I still being unjustly punished for this crime I DID NOT COMMIT?'

Having taken a great involvement in a number of high-profile criminal cases in Britain I was contacted by Reyos in 2004 and have gone on to spend 13 years researching his case.

During my research into Reyos' case I have obtained verbatim copies of documentation upon which I have reached my firm conclusions of what is surely one of the gravest miscarriages of justice in the United States of America. It is a case which has seen an innocent man fighting to clear his name since November 1982 (when he was charged with murder). To put this into context I was born only weeks before Reyos was sent to prison and therefore all I have ever known, all of my life experiences, all of my concept of time is limited to that period during which Reyos has been arguing against something he did not do; a fact which makes me all the more determined to help end this injustice. With this aim in mind I helped establish the Justice for James Harry Reyos campaign, creating a website and have helped publicize his case in the media.

In addition to studying the facts of his case, I have also corresponded extensively with Reyos and spoken to him on the telephone. It is unnecessary for me to meet him, in this case, to be convinced of his innocence; there are sufficient evidential grounds outlined in this book for me to be entirely confident of my conclusion without having to see Reyos in person. I am aware that he has been described, consistently, as a gentle, caring man who is disciplined. He described himself to me as a 'very easygoing and happy person. Despite my wrongful conviction I am still a happy person, not allowing life's setbacks to get me down.' For my own part I have found him to be a thoroughly decent, intelligent, articulate man who likes the quiet life and loves animals, especially cats. He has always been a pleasure to know and I have often made these thoughts known to the Texas Board of Pardons and Paroles, as have a large number of other character referees, but thus far without success. As a Native American his belief system has the 'Great Spirit' at its head and frequently he will express his gratitude to the Great Spirit for the support he has had from me and others.

I like facts to speak for themselves, and indeed in this case they do. However, it is also essential that the reader gains an insight into Reyos, his background, his character and his struggles. As such I have quoted large extracts of Reyos' letters and emails to me. These correspondences show the human dimension of this tragic case. It is ultimately Reyos' story and so I have opted to use his words as much as possible.

It is my hope that you, the reader, will learn much about the failings of the United States justice system, and in particular the Texas justice system which can fail so spectacularly that not only can innocent people be robbed of their liberty, but that it allows murderers to continue to walk the streets.

Scott Lomax
England, December 2017 (Scott_lomax1982@gmail.com)

Please Come Home for Christmas

Priests are the last people expected to go missing during religious festivals, but this is exactly what happened during the Christmas period in 1981 in the small town of Denver City in the state of Texas, USA.

There had been concerns raised about Father Patrick Ryan when he had failed to deliver Midnight Mass at the St William's Roman Catholic Church, on Christmas Eve. Father Ryan was the parish priest for Denver City, with its population of around 5000, and the nearby Plains. When he had failed to deliver Mass on December 23, his congregation had assumed he had been called out to a sick person. However, when he was not present on Christmas Eve concerns began to grow.

In fact Father Ryan, who was much loved and would later be described, by a parish official, as "Saintly" and "very Christ-like", had not been seen since Monday December, 21, which was very out of character. Eventually the head of the men's church group, Angel Perez, climbed through a window of the rectory, which was beside the church, to see if the 49 year old priest was inside. There were fears he might have been ill and needed medical help but the concerns were no greater than that. Perez found no signs of life in the building but was surprised to see a fully cooked and untouched meal of steak and potatoes on a stove.

It was on Christmas Day itself that the police began to appeal for information about the whereabouts of the missing priest, when his disappearance was reported to them. His absence in the run up to Christmas had been considered unusual by his parishioners but his failure to give Mass on Christmas Day itself was highly worrying.

Yoakum County Sheriff, Jim Rice, said, "There was no evidence in the house of any struggle. There was a fully cooked meal prepared and still sitting on the stove." Ryan's 1979 white-over-maroon Chrysler Newport was gone but the priest had seemingly not taken any personal belongings other than his silver chalice and accordion, which he usually took with him when traveling. He had clearly hurriedly left the rectory of his own will, but why he did so was a mystery.

From the outset it was believed Father Ryan may have come to some harm at the hands of someone exploiting his "work for the poor", according to fellow Pallottine priest Reverend Bill Hanly, who had known Ryan since 1949 when they both entered the seminary in Thurles. They were ordained together in 1956 and had celebrated 25 years in the priesthood together during the summer. Hanly firmly believed that a crime of some form had occurred. Ryan often invited people into his home who were homeless and/or needed help. Could one of these individuals have taken advantage of Father Ryan's caring nature? It was a possibility that needed to be considered.

The police tried to keep an open mind, or at least convey an open mind in their public statements. It was announced that they had not ruled out the possibility Father Ryan had become ill, having contracted malaria some years previously whilst carrying out Missionary work in Africa. Could the priest have hurriedly left whilst ill and when his condition deteriorated could he have found it impossible to reach help?

It seemed unlikely and the police soon announced their concerns. Sheriff Rice spoke to the press, saying:

> "At this point everything is speculation. He missed Wednesday night mass, he was absent from midnight mass last night and again at the Christmas noon mass. I am going on the assumption that foul play is involved until something indicates to me there is a different angle to it."

The hope that something would point to a different angle was ended days later, however, when Father Patrick Ryan's fate became known.

Father Patrick Ryan

The Sand and Sage Motel

The Texan city of Odessa, located largely within Ector County but extending also into Midland County, was, in the 1980s, what can be described as a red neck town. Following a succession of oil booms large numbers of people flocked to the city to work. In fact in 1925 only 750 people lived in Odessa, but with the discovery of oil in 1929 this figure rose to 5000 in that year. The population exploded with further oil booms into the 1970s.

The increased population saw a dramatic rise in the level of crime. The solved murder of Betty Williams in 1961, which has come to be known as the Kiss and Tell Murder, is still well remembered. Odessa is the most violent city in Texas, with 806.4 crimes per 100,000 inhabitants according to statistics from 2013.

On Monday December 21, 1981 a man walked into the Sand and Sage Motel on 1213 West Second Street in the town of Odessa, Texas, 94 miles south east of Denver City. Today the building is the Mission Messiah women's shelter, where women go for refuge from domestic violence, but 36 years ago it was the scene of unimaginable brutality.

The man, who was wearing casual slacks and a golf shirt, checked into Room 126 but it later transpired he had given a false name, false address and false car registration plate details. This was not an uncommon occurrence, with the Sand and Sage being a common destination for casual sexual encounters.

It later emerged the man was a practicing homosexual who would cruise the streets for young adult men to have sex with. Indeed it is believed that the man was intending to meet someone for a sexual encounter that night, and had made arrangements to that effect, which was why he was at the motel. He arrived at between 7:30pm and 8pm, according to the motel clerk, N Farr, who said it was "somewhere in that area. It was getting dark out.", but he never checked out. The person he had arranged to meet had more than sex in mind. George Cooper, who was watching television in the adjacent room heard nothing that night to arouse his suspicions. He had checked in at 9pm. The following morning, at around 11am, horror was realized when the cleaning lady entered the room to carry out her cleaning duties and very soon after was running to the manager's office in a state of hysteria.

The woman was instantly struck by the damage throughout the room. Someone had completely trashed the room. The bed was broken and overturned, with the mattress knocked through the frame which had broke, on to the floor. The headboard was splintered. A table was overturned. There was even a large hole in one of the walls. A phone had been ripped from the wall and was completely shattered, as was a television and the air conditioner was badly damaged. The fact that Cooper had not heard anything suggests that the crime was committed before 9pm, though it is still remarkable that nobody else heard anything unusual.

Just inside the door was a wristwatch with a broken strap as if it had been ripped off during a fight. Immediately next to the watch was the body of a man. He was dead, having been so severely beaten with extreme violence that his features could not be easily seen and there was blood everywhere; a pool of blood immediately near the body and stains of dried blood on the walls and on many of the damaged items of furniture.

The man was naked, laying face down, on the floor, with his hands tied very securely behind his back with strips of heavy cloth (some reports claim a sock was used). It would later be shown that he had been sexually assaulted (though this was not publicly mentioned at the time, probably to provide some dignity to the dead man and to spare the feelings of his relatives who were already going through too much) and his head battered with a blunt instrument such as a table leg hours earlier. His neck had been crushed with at least one blow and it was believed the throat injury was the cause of death but that head injuries alone would have caused death. There was a laceration across his buttocks and scratches on his arms. When the State pathologist undertook an examination, arriving at the motel at noon, he estimated death had taken place between twelve and eighteen hours previously.

The victim weighed approximately 200lbs and so detectives thought that whoever killed the unfortunate man must have had tremendous strength to overpower him and tie him up, and it is highly likely he must have been a sizeable person. Of course, there may initially have been a degree of agreement involved; the victim may have consented to have his hands bound together as part of a rough sex game but that did not explain the damage in the room.

"It looked like a struggle took place.", remarked police Lieutenant Kevin R Jones. He later remarked that it appeared "like almost a wrestling match" had taken place. Police Officer Philip Miles remarked that "an out and out fight" had occurred. Indeed it must have been a ferocious struggle involving a violent, strong assailant.

The car, which the victim had arrived in, was no longer in the parking lot outside the motel. With the victim having given false registration details, and the true registration number not known, identifying him through vehicle record checks was not possible. It appeared the man's killer had quietly slipped away after committing the heinous crime and had used his victim's vehicle as his get away car. If he had a vehicle of his own he must have returned later to collect it.

At this early stage the police had little to go on. Not only did they have no idea of who the perpetrator was, they did not know the identity of the victim and only had false details to pursue. The unknown man was taken to the morgue for an autopsy whilst the police tried to figure out his identity.

Late on the Saturday a police officer in Odessa picked up a newspaper and read, with growing interest, a report of a missing priest from Denver City. People go missing all the time, but a priest disappearing during the festive season seemed unusual to the Odessa police. There was nothing in their victim's belongings to suggest he could be a priest but the more the police thought about it, the more it seemed that the murdered John Doe could be the missing clergyman.

Eventually an identification took place, with several members of Father Ryan's flock traveling to Odessa to view the body of the murdered man. They confirmed it was their parish priest who had been killed.

The Sand and Sage Motel, Odessa

Father Patrick Ryan

What do we know about Father Patrick Ryan? Could there be some clue in his life history that could shed some light on why he was murdered in such a brutal manner? Could there be some clues as to why he was at the Sand and Sage Motel and why he felt inclined to use a false identity? Was he hiding a secret that led to his demise?

Father Patrick (or "Paddy" as he was affectionately known) Joseph Ryan was born in Doon, County Limerick in the Republic of Ireland in 1932. As a teenager he received his calling and decided to enter the church as a priest. In order to achieve this he entered, in 1949, St Patrick's College, a Pallottine seminary at Thurles in County Tipperary, and later became a Dean of Studies. He was ordained in 1956.

Following Father Ryan's death he was often described as a man who felt a great need to help those less fortunate. It was for this reason that he spent 12 years on missionary work in Tanzania, working in some of the world's most impoverished communities. Reverend Bill Hanly, who also entered the seminary in Thurles, in 1949, said that Father Ryan "worked constantly to help people."

Having spent 12 years in Africa, Father Ryan moved to the USA. However, there is a gap of several years where his whereabouts are unknown. Those who have researched Father Ryan's life have not been able to piece together his life story for most of the 1970s and those who know him have not assisted in providing any useful information. The annually produced US Official Catholic Directory does not include Father Ryan until 1979. Where in the USA did he live and preach? If he was not preaching during this time, what was he doing? Why is there so much secrecy for this period of Father Ryan's life?

After several years of living in some unknown community or communities, it was in 1979 that the first known record was produced regarding Father Ryan's presence in the USA. In that year the Catholic Directory listed Father Ryan, for the first time, stating he was working in the Amarillo Diocese. He was appointed by Bishop Leroy T. Matthiesen. The now late Bishop Matthiesen consistently claimed he had no recollection of where or how he first met Father Ryan. The following year Father Ryan was appointed pastor of St William's Church in Denver City, Yoakum County, Texas.

The Parish of St William was small, with the town having just 5000 residents. Father Ryan was also the priest for nearby Plains.

Father Ryan was described in media reports, soon after his death, as being "Saintly" and "Christ like" He was a much loved priest and members of his congregation recalled how he gave good sermons and liked to sing. He was also described as being a "friend to everybody." A member of the congregation, Pierre St. Romaine, told the press:

> "Everybody is just shocked. He was such a good, saintly man. He was such a wonderful man. He reminded you of St Francis of Assisi. He wanted to be poor, work with the poor and didn't want anything for himself."

In time, however, it would be revealed that not everyone agreed with the 'Saintly' and 'Christ-like' descriptions of Father Patrick Ryan.

The Police Investigation

Father Ryan had family in the USA, with a sister living in New York and a brother in California. His siblings helped make funeral arrangements, with Reverend C. Ramirez of St Paul's Catholic Church in Seminole, Texas and the father superior of the Catholic Pallottine Order. It was arranged that Father Ryan's body would be flown back to Ireland where he would be buried at St Fintan's Cemetery in Doon. At the funeral Mass, which was held in the USA before the body was flown back to Ireland, Bishop Leroy Matthiesen described Father Ryan as being "yet another martyr", adding, "May his blood, shed by strangers, as with the Saviour, be the seed that springs up new Christians."

There was no doubt that this was a case of violent murder and Jimmy Harris, a Justice of the Peace, ruled the death a homicide, with the blow to the throat having been the fatal injury. Whilst plans were being made for Father Ryan's funeral, the police investigation continued unabated, with new lines of enquiry to explore given that the identity of the victim was now known. Who would want to kill and priest, and why?

Robbery was suspected from the outset to be the motive given the missing car and with no money or wallet being found on the deceased or in the room. "His wallet was gone and his car was gone, so it may be robbery. It could be part of it.", Jones told the press in the days following the identification. The vehicle was later found in Hobbs, New Mexico, where it had been left outside a Moose Hotel since Christmas Eve, three days after the murder. Where had it been for those few days? Forensic specialists were sent to examine the car in the hope of finding further fingerprints, and other evidence, that could identify who had stolen it and who had, presumably, committed the murder. Importantly there was money in the trunk of the car, suggesting that the murder was probably not motivated by money.

When Father Ryan's home was searched his chalice and accordion were missing. As a keen accordion player, Father Ryan used to take it with him if he was staying away from home overnight. He was also believed to take the chalice with him. Neither object was found at the Sand and Sage motel or in Father Ryan's car.

The police concluded these had been stolen by the murderer, perhaps as a trophy or souvenir for the crime. Serial killers, in particular, often take souvenirs from the scenes of their crimes.

It was speculated that Father Ryan had been killed by someone who he had tried to help. When asked why the priest might have visited the motel, Reverend Hanley told the press, "He might have tried to help someone and they took advantage of that." Jones agreed that this was possible, saying, "They said he was a friend to everybody. He could have brought someone down here or something. It's hard to say."

There was no obvious weapon left at the scene, but detectives believed that one of the legs of the damaged table could have been the blunt instrument used to deliver many of the blows. The other injuries were inflicted by the hands, and probably also the feet, of the killer.

Given the amount of damage in the motel room it was debatable how many people were involved. If more than one individual was responsible it would be likely that Father Ryan would have been very quickly overpowered and there would have been little struggle and therefore little damage. However, it is possible that more than one person was involved and that in a fit of rage they broke fixtures and furniture before fleeing. The police considered the possibility that more than one person was behind the crime and soon announced they wanted to speak to two men seen with Father Ryan earlier on the last day he had been seen alive: Monday December 21. One of these men was quickly identified, as the reader will soon discover, whilst the other man has never been identified.

Jones was confident the killer or killers could be quickly apprehended because of the abundance of physical evidence at the scene and in the victim's car. There were lots of hairs on the body which did not belong to Father Ryan. The crime scene and car also contained many bloodstained fingerprints belonging to the killer. A large number of empty beer cans and cigarette butts were strewn across the floor of the motel room, which would have contained fingerprints and traces of saliva. Whether the victim and his killer had drunk together in peaceful circumstances before the crime commenced is unknown. Semen stains and bloodstains were visible on the carpet and bed sheets and could have helped identify the killer, even in the days before DNA analysis.

It would appear the murder had not been premeditated and the killer had been careless or, as we describe it in Britain, 'forensically unaware', not knowing that he was leaving physical evidence that could later be used to identify and convict him. With so many clues, even with more primitive techniques and knowledge of forensic science than exists today, it seemed likely that the police would be able to get their man before long. Certainly the murderer left many clues that should have led the police to secure a quick arrest and a conviction that was correct without a shadow of a doubt.

A man was questioned in connection with the murder when it emerged that he had been with Father Ryan, at his home, on the night before his death and that he was one of the two men who had been seen with Father Ryan hours before his death. That man was James Harry Reyos.

A crime scene photograph showing some of the damage, along with some of the cigarette butts

James Harry Reyos

James Harry Reyos was born on May 25, 1956, and is the youngest of six children. A full-blooded Native American, as a member of the Jicarilla Apache nation, he grew up in a Jicarilla Apache Reservation on a ranch near Chama, in northern New Mexico.

The land occupied by the members of the Jicarilla Apache Nation is located in the rugged, mountainous parts of northern New Mexico, with its pine forests adding to a picturesque landscape. The city of Dulce forms the main settlement of the Jicarilla Apache people. A distinctive form of basket making created by the Jicarilla tribe forms the origin of that name, with Jicarilla meaning 'little basket'.

It is a beautiful part of the country and Reyos speaks warmly of his childhood surroundings, 'It's a pretty state to live.', he once told me, adding that it had 'Very nice weather.'

Although the weather is hot in the summer months, with fields that were 'nice and green', during winter it becomes, in Reyos' words, 'cold.....bone-chilling COLD, down to the MINUS degrees.' Reyos loves the cold weather and jokes about how he ought to move to the North Pole. 'I love the snow, the cold climate.', he once wrote, and he has fond memories of the ice and heavy snow where he grew up. Living in a mobile home the cold weather often made things difficult but Reyos, his family and others living nearby, took it in their stride. One morning Reyos awoke to find that the temperature was minus 30 degrees and that the front screen door to the mobile home would not open, because it was covered with ice two inches in thickness. Throwing his full body weight against it he eventually managed to get it open before helping his dad to get the truck engine heated up so that it would work, before Reyos went to his neighbors to help them with their own mobile homes. Every winter he still loves the cold weather and dreams of spending even colder winters back in New Mexico if granted a pardon. Until then he is not allowed to leave Texas.

Reyos had a very close relationship with his family, in particular his father who he described as his 'beloved dad', and had a cheeky personality as a child, often playing pranks on his siblings.

He realized as a teenager that he was gay but he felt shame because of the conservative values of the tribe. Increasingly he would turn to alcohol to escape from the feelings of guilt and shame.

Despite his drinking and his emotional difficulties Reyos was a model student and did well at school, being a member of the National Honor Society. He went on to university at the University of New Mexico in Albuquerque to study petroleum technology.

Unfortunately alcohol was a vice which began to have a negative impact on his life at this time, as his drinking got out of control. Away from his family and the conservative views of his tribe, and with the access to alcohol and attitudes towards it amongst student populations, Reyos began to drink heavily. He later stated that his drinking was largely in an attempt to "suppress the gay feelings that I had."

In 1977 Reyos had to leave university due to his father having a serious accident and he was required to work on the ranch but he continued his education at the Eastern New Mexico State University.

In 1980 Reyos was banned from the dorm on account of his excessive drinking and associated reckless behavior, which resulted in frequent encounters with the police. He was arrested more than thirty times for drunken behavior and had been banned from driving on five occasions. His life was a mess and one of self-destruction although he showed no signs of violence. None of his arrests had involved aggressive or violent behavior. During this time he spent all his spare money on alcohol

It was Reyos' drinking that resulted in him encountering a man who would change his life forever.

On December 6, 1981 Reyos, then aged 25, had just lost his job as an oilfield roustabout with Mobil in Denver City on account of being drunk at work. He decided to walk to Hobbs where he could look for work. Hobbs was approximately a half hour's drive from Denver City, where Reyos had been living for the past eight months.

Reyos was hoping to hitch a ride and after a little while a vehicle pulled up beside him. Reyos was relieved to have a lift and thanked the casually dressed driver who introduced himself as John. As they talked it emerged they were near neighbors, living only two blocks apart, although they had never met before. It was a chance meeting which was to take Reyos on a journey towards jail.

John took Reyos to a Tipp's Inn and they both drank beer and vodka and chatted for around five hours. Reyos liked the man, who he later learned was using a false name. During their drinking session the man calling himself John had not spoken about his work, and Reyos does not recall religion being a topic of discussion. Reyos only learnt he was a man of the cloth when John dropped him off outside the rectory. He did not learn that the man was in fact named Father Patrick Ryan until after the murder, instead calling him Father John.

Reyos would later describe 'Father John', as being "kind and considerate" and indeed the priest lent Reyos some money and tried to befriend the troubled man. Reyos regarded Ryan as a sort of mentor who lent a sympathetic ear. As a Native American it was an unusual friendship, with the two men unlikely to cross paths in ordinary circumstances, but time would quickly show they had something in common, in addition to their fondness for heavy drinking, which they both liked to keep hidden: their sexuality.

Reyos thought of the clergyman as a friend. However, an unpleasant side, far removed from the behavior associated with the priesthood, soon emerged one evening when Reyos paid Ryan a visit.

It was on December 20, the day before Ryan's death, that Reyos was asked to visit the rectory and bring over a photo album. Ryan had expressed an interest in Reyos' family, saying he was fascinated by Native American culture and wanted to learn more about his heritage. Reyos obliged (he is a proud Native American with a deep love for the lands of the Jicarilla Apache tribe) and the two men began drinking beer whilst looking over the photographs. Reyos also took some audio cassettes, with country music he had recorded from the radio.

The encounter seemed friendly and the men began drinking vodka and orange juice and also whisky, but things quickly changed. Reyos later testified at his murder trial:

> "I was sitting down there on the chair, and Father Ryan came up to me, grabbed me by the, by the shirt collar. And I, he pulled me toward him and had me perform oral sex on him."

Ryan was significantly stronger than Reyos, with more than a 75lb difference in weight, and his struggle was unsuccessful.

According to Reyos, as quoted in the *Austin Chronicle*, he was ashamed by the encounter and quickly left. "I didn't even grab my stuff. I was walking down the street thinking, 'That didn't happen; that couldn't happen'."

It has been argued that Reyos did in fact consent to this sexual favor but was so ashamed of his own sexual orientation, having never been openly homosexual, that it was easier for him to believe he was sexually assaulted.

Reyos is adamant that he did not consent and that he was sexually assaulted. He told me:

> 'I do forgive Father Ryan for sexually assaulting me. In order to have peace of mind -- and to comply with the Great Spirit's teaching on "forgiveness," I must forgive – it's imperative to forgive him. Sure, the emotional hurt will never go away, but I want to know, in my heart, that I have forgiven him.'

Whether or not there was consent, Reyos fled, leaving his backpack and photo album behind. The following night Father Ryan was murdered in the seedy motel room, having again used a false name.

It was the backpack and photo album which were to result in James Harry Reyos first coming to the attention of the investigation.

A Native American sculpture in El Paso (Photograph taken by James Harry Reyos)

A Native American quilt (photograph taken by James Harry Reyos)

Reyos Emerges as a Suspect

Five days after the murder, once Father Ryan had been identified, the rectory was searched and Reyos' backpack and photo album were found, with the police quickly able to identify their owner. They were greatly assisted by the fact that the album contained Reyos' high school diploma.

Reyos was taken in for questioning and admitted he had been at Father Ryan's home the day before the killing. He also admitted having been one of the two men seen with Father Ryan earlier on the day of the crime itself. He informed the police that the other man was a hitchhiker and he gave a description of the man, and details of where he was taken (these details are outlined in a later chapter of this book).

Reyos denied any involvement in the murder, claiming to have an alibi, which the police investigated and found corroborating evidence for. In fact Reyos provided the police officers with a number of receipts and a speeding ticket which showed he was 200 miles away, in Roswell, on the night of the murder.

Had Reyos been involved in the murder, and the "out and out fight", as it was described by the police, there should have been bruises, scratches and other marks on him. There were none when Reyos removed his clothing to be examined by Police Officer Jerry Smith on December 26. There was a very small cut on one of Reyos' hands, but this was not considered suspicious. The police knew that if Reyos was guilty then Ryan could not have put up a fight. However, that was clearly not the case because of the damage caused in different parts of the room and the blood staining found across the room. Even if Reyos had killed Father Ryan, and then, in a rage, caused large amounts of damage, there would still have been cuts and bruises upon his hands.

Reyos' fingerprints, and hair and saliva samples he gave, did not match those found at the crime scene or any traces that were found at the wheel of Father Ryan's vehicle. Reyos did not smoke, which is important when considering the large number of cigarette butts at the crime scene. According to Reyos, Father Ryan was not a heavy smoker. Reyos claims that during the several hours they spent together during their first meeting Father Ryan only smoked one or two cigarettes and while they were together on the evening of December 20, Father Ryan did not smoke at all. If true then Father Ryan was highly anxious so much so that he smoked many cigarettes on his own, or both he and the killer smoked.

Reyos' apartment was searched for the chalice and accordion which were missing from the rectory. Neither of these objects were found amongst Reyos' belongings.

Finally, Reyos volunteered to take a polygraph test, six days after the murder. During the test he vehemently denied any involved any murder and he maintained that position throughout questioning. Although polygraph tests are not infallible, it was accepted that Reyos was telling the truth. Detective Jerry Smith, the primary Odessa Police Department investigator, wrote in a report, 'At about 5:30 p.m., Det. Casey completed Reyos polygraph. Det. Casey advised that he felt like Reyos was truthful and was not involved in the homicide.'

With all of the above considered the police accepted Reyos was not involved in Father Ryan's murder, and they released him.

With Reyos free to go, the investigation continued. However, the police struggled to find the individual responsible for the horrific murder, with no witnesses having seen or heard anything suspicious on the night of Father Ryan's death. Almost one year on, when hopes of bringing the killer to justice were fading, a surprise phone call gave police the breakthrough they were wanting.

A Phone Call

As the months passed, almost a year after the crime, the murder had ceased to be mentioned in the newspapers but it was still very much at the forefront of the minds of those who knew Father Patrick Ryan. The police in Odessa still hoped to catch the man responsible but other crimes had taken place and resources had to be spent investigating those crimes. The murder investigation was eventually scaled down so much so that there was no active investigation by November 1982.

During 1982 a man moved around West Texas and New Mexico, not settling anywhere for long though he lived for a short time in Memphis before returning, on November 9, 1982, to Albuquerque where he stayed in a run down Bow and Arrow Lodge.

The man was a heavy drinker and on his first night in Albuquerque he was arrested for public drunkenness. Taken into custody the man told officers "I may have killed a priest in West Texas."

There were concerns about the man's state of mind, and it was thought he was hallucinating and in a state of serious mental distress, and so he was admitted into the county mental health facility. During his stay he was visited by the police, but he refused to answer any of their questions although the police were able to establish his identity: James Harry Reyos.

Uncertain about the reliability of the story, and recognizing Reyos' drunken behavior and evident confusion it was causing, which did include hallucinations, the police did not believe he was the killer. No doubt their conclusion was also based upon the earlier investigation into Reyos, just days after the murder, which had concluded he was innocent. Reyos was released from the facility and returned to his hotel, having been diagnosed as an alcoholic.

Soon later, on November 18, following a weeklong binge of pills (Quaaludes) and alcohol, Reyos staggered to a public phone and dialed 911, telling the dispatcher, Dolly Woody, that he wanted to talk to someone about "the killing of a Catholic priest in Odessa, Texas." When asked who he was, and why he needed to speak to officers involved in the murder investigation, he responded, "You are talking to the killer."

He went on to say that he beat Father Ryan and slashed him with a razor. Although Ryan's buttocks had been lacerated this was common knowledge and not something only the killer would know.

A patrol car was sent to the Bow and Arrow Lodge to arrest Reyos. The police would later claim, at Reyos' trial, that their suspect was not overly drunk, with only a slight odor of alcohol detected. This would appear to have been an attempt to mislead the jury because it was clear to the dispatcher that Reyos had indeed been heavily under the influence of drink and the tape recording of Reyos' phone call, which was played to the jury at Reyos' trial, shows him to have been confused, and slurring in his speech, often repeating himself and failing to understand many of the questions put to him.

Upon arriving at the police station, having been arrested, he was appointed a public attorney and immediately retracted his confession, saying, "In the name of God, I didn't do this." He also told the police, "I am not the killer, I just like to cause trouble for law enforcement." His retraction achieved nothing and he was promptly charged with the murder and sent to jail to await trial.

It is an unfortunate aspect of many crimes, especially high-profile murders, that people feel the need to confess to murders they did not commit. Did Reyos admit to a crime he did not commit? Or was he hiding a dark secret which, under the influence of drink and drugs, he was unable to contain?

The Trial

After being charged with murder Reyos spent seven months at Ector County Jail awaiting his trial. He later described to me this time as being, 'Very nerve-racking, filled with anxiety, and lonely. I did not know what to expect, but I was still confident I would be found Not Guilty.'

Locked away from his family and friends, his liberty deprived, Reyos struggled tremendously in coping. Not only did he risk life in prison for a crime he maintained he was not involved in, but he also feared that some of the other prisoners would harm him, maybe even kill him, on account of his homosexuality and the belief he had murdered a priest.

Reyos told me about these fears:

> 'I was somewhat worried about my own safety. The victim was a Catholic priest, so I had death threats placed against me. ... I was removed from general population to protective custody because of the threats, and placed in a cell all by myself. That is where, and when, the loneliness set in.'

Having been charged with one murder he had not committed he also had fears that he would be charged, and tried, with other murders. He told me:

> 'During that time that were a few murders involving Catholic priests, and being that Albuquerque has a large Hispanic population many thought that I was responsible for some of the murders. As a matter of fact, after my arrest, I was questioned about the murder of Father Reynaldo Rivera from Santa Fe, New Mexico. Police detectives from Santa Fe traveled to Albuquerque to question me. Of course, I had nothing to do with his murder and they released me as a suspect and went back to Santa Fe to resume their investigation of his murder.'

The murder of Father Reynaldo Rivera remains unsolved to this day, as do the murders of a number of other priests, and these are discussed in later chapters in order to see whether there may be any connection between these crimes and Father Ryan's murder.

Reyos' trial was scheduled to take place in June 1983 and so for a period of seven months Reyos remained his small cell knowing his fate rested in the hands of twelve individuals who had never met him. He hoped they would see what the police had originally known, that all the evidence suggested he was not responsible for the terrible crime.

The trial took place at the Ector County Courthouse and lasted four days. It is incredible that a man's liberty can be decided upon in such a hurried manner, with evidence not being satisfactorily questioned. The evidence will be detailed in the chapters which follow, but the evidence against him was largely based upon his confession and his known association with the victim.

Throughout his evidence Reyos struggled with his testimony. This was in part because of the shock of the experience, the high price at stake and because he had to testify that he was gay in front of his father and one of his sisters, who he had never been open to about his sexuality. He broke down in tears when asked if he was gay. At first he refused to answer the question, replying, "I will not admit that I am, nor do I deny it." He was afraid to acknowledge his sexuality in the presence of his father. However, this gave the jury the impression he was evasive. Eventually he told the court he was gay, at which time his father walked up to him in the court, hugged him and told Reyos that he accepted him for whoever and whatever he was. It was a moving experience for Reyos but even though his father accepted him for whatever he was, Reyos believes the jury saw a homosexual, alcoholic Native American. In a Red Neck town such as Odessa he felt sure that the jury were not going to look at the evidence in sufficient detail, and would be distracted by their attitudes towards aspects of Reyos' personality. Time would tell, as is later shown in this book, that Reyos' fears were justified, with a member of the jury confirming that they were influenced by Reyos' "characteristics". He was terrified that they would therefore decide in their minds that he must also be a priest killer.

The key aspects of the evidence will be discussed in the following few chapters to show the prosecution's case and how the facts stack up to show that a grave error has been made in the hunt for Father Ryan's killer.

The Confession

Why did Reyos confess to the murder if he had nothing to do with it? The confession formed the key evidence against him and so it is essential to understand why he told the police he was responsible.

The fact Reyos had an alibi should have been enough to demonstrate to the jury that he could not have been responsible for the murder. However, the confession was an issue that the jury could not get past. Following the trial a member of the jury came forward to claim that they began their deliberations on the assumption that Reyos was guilty, because why otherwise would he confess to the crime? On another occasion a member of the jury, who may or may not be the same individual, told the Odessa American that they convicted Reyos "based on his confession and characteristics." If true this highlights a major problem in the case because a jury is supposed to begin deliberations on the assumption that a defendant is innocent until they can find sufficient ground to prove, beyond reasonable doubt, that the defendant is guilty. The jury seems to have carried out their duty in reverse order. However, it is understandable that a jury would struggle to understand Reyos' confession.

In Texas law a confession alone, even if retracted, is sufficient evidence to allow a prosecution and can result in a conviction. Yet Reyos' confession did not contain any information which only the killer could know. For example, Reyos' confession did not make any reference to Father Ryan being bound or sexually assaulted, it did not provide any detailed description of the injuries inflicted and it did not give any explanation as to how Reyos disposed of the priest's vehicle. There is also a credible argument to suggest it was unreliable and untruthful.

It is suggested that Reyos felt guilt for Father Ryan's murder. Earlier on that day in December 1981 he had been with Father Ryan and had asked the priest to take him to pick up his vehicle. Reyos believes that if he had not asked Father Ryan for a lift, he may not have met his killer and could still be alive. Importantly, it has been argued, the sexual encounter between Reyos and Father Ryan caused shame which led to a great feeling of guilt on Reyos' part. This left Reyos feeling guilt which psychologists believe, with the influence of drugs and alcohol, may have led him to claim responsibility for something he did not do. Reyos himself has said, "I was pretty disorientated in and out of knowing what was going on." In fact during a number of his heavy drinking episodes from his student days onwards, which had resulted in arrests for public disorder, Reyos had been believed to hallucinate and had difficulty distinguishing imagination and reality.

It is not surprising that Reyos felt disorientated, due to the drugs he had taken before making his confession. Quaalude pills are the brand name for methaqualone, a sleeping drug renowned for its sedative and hypnotic properties, which was popular during the 1970s and early 1980s, until its manufacture was discontinued in 1985. In 1982 it was a legal drug. Taken in large quantities, and particularly combined with alcohol, these pills can cause delirium. As such they alter a person's state of mind and the words spoken by that individual should not be considered reliable.

At trial Dr Samuel Roll, Professor of Psychology and Psychiatry of the University of New Mexico, who specialized in forensic psychology, testified that the confession was not truthful. The following testimony is taken verbatim from the trial transcripts (volume 8, p28):

'Q. [Defense Attorney] Doctor, based on having listened to all of these statements that Mr. Reyos made in Albuquerque on the 18th and 19th of [November 1982] and based on your background and experience in studying the area of false confessions, do you have an opinion based on reasonable scientific certainty as to whether or not the confession by Mr. Reyos to killing Father Ryan was a true confession or a false confession?
A. [Dr. Samuel Roll, professor of psychology and psychiatry and an expert in forensic psychology from the University of New Mexico] Yes, I do have.
Q. What is your opinion?
A. My opinion is that the confession that Mr. Reyos made to killing Father Ryan is a false confession, and that is my opinion with a high degree of scientific certainty.
Q. Is it your opinion then, Doctor, based on reasonable scientific certainty that Mr. Reyos, based on your tests and evaluations and

background, did – is it your opinion that it was likely or unlikely that he could commit a crime of this nature?

A. It is my opinion that it would be extremely unlikely that Mr. Reyos would be capable of committing a crime of this nature.'

It was the expert's opinion that Reyos was a "dystonic homosexual" who felt guilt and shame about his sexual orientation. Fuelled by alcohol and drugs Reyos was driven to make a false confession, according to Roll. He believed that Reyos had broken several taboos of his tribe, including having sex with a male, in particular a religious man and one of a different culture, and therefore he felt tremendous guilt and shame. With feelings of shame and guilt, according to Roll, Reyos would have felt the need to confess to having done something. Roll felt that Reyos would, at a time when he was not thinking clearly due to drink and drugs, rather confess to being a killer in which he could claim sex was not consensual, but that a sexual assault had taken place, rather than admit he was homosexual. Roll has been quoted as saying, "All the characteristics are there that you would expect in a false confession."

At the trial Roll gave a number of examples of individuals giving false confessions, including a man who confessed to a rape rather than admit that he had stolen a pair of shoes (so that he could have sex with the shoes). In that case the offender felt rape was a more socially acceptable crime.

It may still be difficulty for some people to believe that a man could feel so inadequate in himself, and ashamed of himself, that he could create such a lie and make a confession without being prompted to do so, which was entirely untruthful. Reyos was not physically or emotionally bullied or pressured in any way by law enforcement officers into making his confession. There is no suggestion that he was subject to police brutality. Instead he confessed voluntarily. To further explain why Reyos may have confessed to a crime he did not commit I will recount the details of a case from Britain where a man who was entirely innocent of the murder of a young girl confessed to killing her.

In June 1972 a 14 year old girl was murdered near her home in Tamworth. The girl, named Julia Roberts, had been riding her bike along country lanes on the evening of 7 June. Her body was discovered in a field the following day and it was apparent she had been sexually assaulted.

A major investigation followed, with thousands of men questioned, but the police could not link anyone to the crime.

Things would change a few months later, however, when the police began to concentrate their resources on a soldier named Andrew Evans. Evans had been suffering with depression for some time, and had been prescribed valium a few weeks before the police questioned him.

On the evening of Sunday 8 October 1972 officers investigating the murder visited Evans at his grandmother's home. He had been routinely questioned before, as one of the thousands of men in the area, and had given police the names of three other soldiers who could provide alibis. However, it transpired that two of the three soldiers had not been serving at the barracks by the time of the murder, and they had been unable to locate the third soldier. As such there was no one who could corroborate Evans' story.

Although Evans wrote a statement in which he reiterated his claim that he had been in the barracks at the time of the murder, he was highly disturbed by the questioning and began to question whether he had been involved in the crime. Although he did not suggest he had been the killer, whilst the police were present, he did ask the officers what would happen to the murderer if he was caught. The response given was that the killer would be in considerable trouble and would need his head examining. After the police left his grandmother spent much of the evening attempting to reassure the worried man, who was by this stage very worked up and agitated, that he had not killed the teenager. This did not, however, prevent him from visiting the police the following day after a sleepless night.

The following morning Evans told his grandmother that he needed to speak to the police and see a photograph of the victim in order to try and recall whether he was responsible for her death. When he arrived at the police station at around 3pm he told a police cadet that he kept dreaming about a girl. When taken to see a Detective Sergeant, Evans was inconsolable, sat with his head between his knees and his hands on his face.

When he had calmed down he told the detective he needed to see a photograph of the victim, adding: "I was in the Army, I don't remember where I was."

After being asked more questions, he was taken to see a Detective Inspector whom he told he was very upset because: "It is this girl who was murdered at Tamworth. I keep seeing a face. I want to see a picture of her. I keep seeing her face. I wonder if I've done it."

Evans was then asked details about the crime and the victim. He provided vague details of the girls face but a very inaccurate description of her clothing. Upon being asked whether he believed he had "done it", the now suspect announced "I don't know whether I've done it or not. ..." Asked whether he had ever been to Tamworth, he replied, "I don't know. I don't know. I could have done. I forget where I've been. I can go down streets and in houses and later I wonder how I got there."

He was then asked about his activities after leaving the army, to which he replied:

> "You see, I can't remember. This is how I am. I could have got home the next day. I don't know where I've been. That is why I keep wondering if it's me that's done this murder. Can you show me a picture to see if I've ever met her?"

He was then asked again if he had killed Judith Roberts, responding "This is it. I don't know. Show me a picture and I'll tell you if I've ever seen her."

At 3:30pm the interview ended, though he remained at the police station and was questioned at 4:15pm by a Detective Chief Inspector and a Detective Constable. He reiterated his demand to see a photograph of the girl but this time announced he believed he had killed the victim: "I keep seeing her face all the time. I can't sleep. I've got to know if I did it because I think I must have done".

"I must have killed her", he later repeated in a hysterical state. Soon afterwards Evans was cautioned and taken to Tamworth Police Station. Whilst at Tamworth he was questioned by one of the detectives who had visited him at his grandmother's home. He was asked by the Detective Sergeant whether he was the killer.

"I think so. I must have done because I can see a picture of her. I can see her lying near to a hedge. I can see her brown hair and she has got a mark across her face", he replied. The mark, he believed, was a wound with blood. Evans then, in a confused state, claimed he had not committed the crime but he may have witnessed the attack and he offered a description of a man he said was the killer, telling the detective it was a small youth around 5'4" in height with dark hair.

He was asked a series of questions, his responses being accurate in some cases but largely inaccurate. He drew a picture of the crime scene which bore no resemblance to the field and showed the victim lying on her back.

The following day he told officers, whilst not under caution, he had dragged the victim from her bicycle and that there had been a struggle, adding that he believed he may have put the bicycle in the hedge.

Shortly afterwards he told detectives "I am sure I killed her.", before asking them in a confused state, "Do you think I did it?"

Later in the afternoon he told an officer, "I know I did it. I've put it down.", before giving the officer three sheets of paper with detailed descriptions and drawings of the crime. The account gave information about a struggle with the girl and reiterated his inaccurate belief that she had been laying on her back. Late that night he provided a further four sheets of paper containing details of his belief of his actions on the fateful day. He was transferred to Litchfield Police Station and questioned about the contents of the sheets of paper, providing a detailed description of the weapon he allegedly used in the attack.

The following day Evans provided two more sheets which included a picture of a girl with no face. He added that the girl had had no clothes on after the attack and that he had left the victim under the hedge, when in reality she was half clothed and had been left near the hedge, under hedge clippings.

During later police questioning it is alleged he provided details of the girls' appearance which only the killer, or someone who had been given information, could know. This was, for the police, sufficient evidence of his guilt despite the largely inaccurate information he had provided and his general confusion about his involvement in the crime. He was taken on a reconstruction of the movements he believed he made on the day of the murder, by a Detective Sergeant from the Metropolitan Police, whom he told: "I want all this cleared up. If I don't receive some treatment I may do it again. I don't want that to happen". Evans appeared to know the area around Robinson's field reasonably well, though he later accounted for this by saying he had been running in the area during training with the army. A detailed confession was provided by Evans, although many of the details were found to be inaccurate.

He decided that a truth drug be used to uncover information that Evans had appeared to have forgotten. Both the defense and prosecution teams agreed that this be an appropriate course of action. Barbiturate drugs were administered, followed by intense questioning, on Friday 30 March 1973. During the course of this action Evans said he had been at the barracks throughout the day of the murder. He did however say that he had witnessed a man standing over the body of Judith Roberts. He described barbed wire and a sign and recalled the name "Brookes." When asked if he killed Judith Roberts he answered "I don't know" and "I didn't do it", before saying "I must find out" and questioning "Was it me?"

A few days later, on 2 April, he was injected with Brietal and given Methedrine, with the hope that it would generate thoughts and improve recollection. Yet again he told detectives he had not left the barracks all day but admitted he knew the area where the crime was committed, but only because police officers had taken him there and because he had been there during his military training. He said he had never seen the victim and had played no role in her death. Against the advice of Dr Washbrook, a third session was undertaken in which Evans gave a detailed description of a man who he said was the killer.

Evans was charged with the murder and despite retracting his confession he stood trial, and was convicted. There were many people convinced that a miscarriage of justice had taken place and campaigned for his release. Eventually evidence began to emerge that Evan's conviction could have been wrong.

In October 1997 a report commissioned by the prosecution for the appeal hearing, written by Dr Joseph, stated:

> 'I believe that when the appellant [Evans] was in the police station on Monday, 9th October 1972 onwards, he was in a highly abnormal mental state. When he described "seeing" the face of the dead girl I believe he is describing what would be categorized as a pseudo-hallucination, namely an abnormal perceptual experience ... I believe that the appellant was in a markedly anxious and "hysterical" frame of mind and it is not

uncommon in such a state for a sufferer to believe that they can see things. ... Taking into account the appellant's abnormal mental state and the way he was presenting himself at the police station, if I had been the psychiatrist examining him at that time or soon afterwards, I would have started off from the basic premise that the "memory" and imagery that he was describing were false and not true. I believe however that the psychiatrists who saw him at that time started from the opposite premise, namely that the memory and imagery the appellant was describing were true but incomplete.'

Dr Joseph further reported that Evans:

'has a tendency to confabulate to fill in gaps in his memory, and the effect of psychiatric intervention at that time was to reinforce the belief that he was suppressing a real memory rather than what I believe to have been the correct analysis, namely that he had been experiencing a pseudo-hallucination and false memory as part of his extreme anxiety and "hysterical" state, which he subsequently elaborated with police and psychiatric encouragement. I believe therefore that his confession is unreliable.'

Dr Joseph's view was shared by three other experts in the field and the appeal judges who, in their judgment, found that the confessions were "entirely unreliable."

The appeal raised many, many contradictions between Evans' account and what actually happened. Evans was wrong in his description of the direction in which Judith was cycling. He was wrong in his claim that he had dragged Judith off her bicycle and across rough terrain, for the killer did not do this. He was wrong in saying that he struck a blow to her head and continued struggling with her, because the medical evidence proved that the first blow had killed her outright. He was wrong in his description of the murder weapon. He was wrong in saying that he inflicted all of the blows when Judith was on the ground, because the medical evidence showed she was stood up when the first blow was struck. He was wrong about where in the field the attack took place. He was wrong about undressing the victim and putting her shoes in her underclothes. He neglected to give any description of hiding the body under hedge clippings and plastic fertilizer bags, despite giving several detailed accounts of his alleged behavior. And he gave inaccurate information about the appearance of his alleged victim and the clothes she was wearing. Whilst some of his information was accurate, it was not a difficult task undermining his confessions, and it has been suggested he obtained information from the police by the questions they asked him.

The similarities between Evan's case and that of James Harry Reyos are staggering. Both were depressed individuals who were prone to episodes of heightened mental state during which they would hallucinate. In this unusual state, which can be exacerbated by stimulants such as alcohol or drugs, it is often impossible to distinguish reality from imagination and when a suggestion is made, from a police officer, that a person could be responsible for a crime then that person will start to question whether there is any truth in that suggestion. In this state of confusion a person can begin to believe that they may have committed the crime in question and therefore make a false confession.

There is no doubt that Evans was innocent of the murder of Judith Roberts and provided a false confession. Could the same be true for Reyos?

Interestingly, two other men confessed to the murder of Father Ryan. Both confessions were dismissed by the police, who believed that the confessors were mentally ill. Yet by the time Reyos' confession, it is claimed, the police needed a conviction and were less willing to dismiss Reyos' words, even if other evidence pointed towards his innocence.

Motive

I believe that all humans are capable of committing a murder of any level of violence if driven to it, unless physical disability prevents them from being able to do so. Reyos certainly had motive to commit the murder; he claimed to have been sexually assaulted by Father Ryan the day before the crime, but was this sufficient to cause him to kill? Did Reyos lure Father Ryan to the Sand and Sage motel under the pretence of a sexual rendezvous in order to kill the priest?

Why, if Reyos had been sexually assaulted, did he return to Father Ryan's home the following day? Did he in fact consent? Was Reyos struggling with his sexuality so much so that he believed he was sexually assaulted? According to Reyos, when he went to Father Ryan's door on the morning of December 21, the priest apologized for what he had done, to which Reyos responded, "Don't worry about it. Forget about it." Therefore was it consensual or was Reyos so in need of a lift to get his truck back that he was willing to take that journey with his attacker? Or was he still in some state of confusion over what had happened? I think the latter is most likely the case. Reyos later described the encounter with Father Ryan as being "surreal" and his recollection was somewhat hazy on account of the amount of alcohol he had consumed.

However, to explore alternative possibilities, did he meet Father Ryan at the Sand and Sage Motel, having agreed to meet him earlier that day, where they had consensual sex? Could Reyos then, upon having sex, felt a great sense of shame, in his struggles with his sexuality, and lashed out in anger?

It would be strange for Reyos to have met Father Ryan at the Sand and Sage Motel when they had already had a sexual encounter at Father Ryan's rectory. Why would Father Ryan arrange to have sex with Reyos in Odessa when they lived so close to one another and would not have been disturbed?

Could others who equally had a motive to kill Father Ryan? Evidence at Reyos' trial did show that Father Ryan was somewhat of a sexual predator, driving the streets looking for young men to have sex with.

There was ample evidence to support Reyos' claim that Father Ryan was a homosexual who preyed on young men. Indeed two witnesses, named Mike Castaneda and Edward Neher, testified at Reyos' trial that they had been approached by Father Ryan outside a grocery store in Hobbs during the spring of 1981. The priest allegedly told the men that he was looking for "a young stud to fuck him" but despite three men all stating on oath that Father Ryan was a sexual predator the jury could not seemingly believe that a clergyman described as being 'Saintly' could be capable of such a thing. Interestingly some of Father Ryan's fellow clergy, who knew him well, have campaigned for Reyos' release, which I consider to be very suggestive that they knew of Father Ryan's behavior.

If he sexually assaulted Reyos, as Reyos alleges, then could Father Ryan not have done the same to another man, or men, who decided to respond with murder? Father Ryan met a man at the Sand and Sage, almost certainly for sex, and the killer almost certainly killed Father Ryan as part of a sex crime, for sexual gratification or as a response to sexual shame, rather than a murder for financial gain.

After all, Father Ryan's vehicle was found a few days after the murder. The short-term use of a vehicle is not sufficient to meet a man and kill him in such a manner. Father Ryan's silver chalice and accordion were both missing, which may have been stolen from Father Ryan's vehicle. It is presumed he took these with him to the Sand and Sage Motel (because they were not at his home) but they were nowhere to be found. A search of Reyos' home failed to locate them. Did the killer remove them as a trophy or souvenir of his crime? Or to sell?

Father Ryan's wallet was missing, of course, and so money may have played a role but it was not the primary reason for this crime. The person, or persons, responsible carried out such violence and damage that there was personal hatred towards the victim.

If indeed Reyos was sexually assaulted, as he claims, then he arguably had a motive to commit the murder, feeling anger towards Father Ryan, but he then returned to see Father Ryan, and ask him for a lift, the following morning. This either indicates his level of anger and feeling of violation was not so high, or there was a very calculated plan on Reyos' part to commit murder. The level of violence in Father Ryan's murder goes against the character of a man who had never previously, and has never since, displayed any violent behavior.

Reyos argues that he had no motive and has forgiven Father Ryan for his crime:

> 'I believe that Father Ryan's own aggressive sexual behavior led to his demise. I do forgive Father Ryan for sexually assaulting me. In order to have peace of mind – and to comply with the Great Spirit's teaching on "forgiveness" I must forgive – it's imperative to forgive him. Sure, the emotional hurt will never go away but I want to know, in my heart, that I have forgiven him.'

Even if, arguably, Reyos had a motive, did he have the means and opportunity?

Reyos' Movements

Both Father Ryan's movements, and those of Reyos on the day of the murder, were discussed during the trial in order to establish whether Reyos could have been at the Sand and Sage Motel when Father Ryan was killed. The information presented, when fully considered, proves beyond all doubt that Reyos could not have been Father Ryan's murderer, yet the jury chose not to accept it.

Angel Perez, the head of the church men's group, who was referred to earlier, testified that at approximately 11:30 on the morning of December 21, 1981 he met Father Ryan "ten miles west of Denver City ... going towards Hobbs ... with two guys in the car." Reyos was indeed one of the men, whilst the second man was a hitchhiker who they had picked up just west of Denver City.

Reyos has never denied being with Ryan early in the day of the murder. Perhaps suggesting that Reyos did initially consent to the sex act with Father Ryan on the previous evening, he returned to Ryan's home on that fatal December day, at around 9am. Reyos had been to the post office in Denver City at 8am to collect his mail and had unexpectedly received a check, from his father, for $750; his quarterly share of a payment for mineral extraction from the reservation. The money was much needed and Reyos must have been greatly relieved. He could now pick up his truck from a bail bondsman named Charlie Bostick who had impounded it as collateral for a charge of driving without a valid license (Reyos' license had been taken away due to a driving offence).

Reyos faced a problem though because the truck was impounded in Hobbs, which was around 30 miles away, and so he needed someone to give him a lift. Not having any friends or family in Denver City, Reyos made the decision to ask Father Ryan for help. After the priest allegedly apologized for what he did, Father Ryan agreed to drive to Hobbs and the pair arrived at the bondsman's house, which also served as his office, at around 11:30am, picking up a hitchhiker along the way. After arriving at Bostick's house, according to Reyos, he never saw Father Ryan again.

Reyos entered the house but was told by the man's daughter that Bostick had gone to the city jail. Reyos left the house but was surprised to see that Father Ryan had driven off without waiting, along with the hitchhiker. Father Ryan's departure was observed by Bostick's daughter. Annoyed by this, Reyos used City Taxi Company to get a taxi from Taco Villa, which was near Bostick's house, to the city jail but by the time Reyos had arrived there, to his dismay, he was told the bondsman had returned home. Reyos got the same taxi back to Bostick's house and finally managed to speak with him at around noon and secured his vehicle, paying the bondsman for its release. Bostick would later confirm that Reyos was alone and that at no point in time had he seen Father Ryan or the priest's vehicle. The men had engaged in a conversation about the truck and about job hunting. He was able to give details of the time at which Reyos had been present. The taxi driver was also able to confirm the time at which he dropped Reyos at Bostick's house.

Having got his truck Reyos bought a case of beer at a Tipp's Inn where he met an acquaintance named Harold who he drank with. Reyos gave Harold a lift home, but they stopped off en route at Levy's Auto Parts Center in Hobbs where Reyos bought gas and a new gas cap. He collected and kept his receipt which had the date and time of the purchase clearly marked upon it. Reyos then drove to Harold's home, arriving at around 1:30pm. Having arrived at Harold's home, Reyos stayed a short while, as confirmed by Harold, who died before the trial but did give a statement.

After driving away from Harold's home, Reyos headed towards Albuquerque to go onto the highway to Dulce in order to spend the festive period with his family. Although a Native American, Reyos has always believed in the significance of Christmas even if he does not believe in the birth of Christ.

En route to Albuquerque, close to Artesia, Reyos says he saw the same hitchhiker who Father Ryan had picked up earlier in the day, and Reyos agreed to give him a lift. Reyos claims that the hitchhiker informed him that Father Ryan had pulled over a few blocks away from Bostick's house and had told him to get out. Father Ryan had then driven away. Reyos agreed to drive the hitchhiker to Roswell bus station.

En-route to Roswell, at 3:30pm (local time: New Mexico is in a time zone one hour behind the time zone which includes Texas), Reyos bought gas at a Mobil station in Artesia, New Mexico, and kept his receipt with the date and time. He then proceeded to Roswell, which is 200 miles from Odessa.

According to Reyos, he and the hitchhiker arrived at Roswell bus station at around 5pm (local time). At that time a bus ticket was sold to a black man traveling to Clinton, Oklahoma.

The hitchhiker has never been identified. Although he is unlikely to have been involved in the murder he was one of the last men to see Father Ryan alive and he could have some useful information. Reyos told me about this hitchhiker:

> 'The hitchhiker who accompanied Father Ryan and I to Hobbs was a black guy, middle age, approx 5'7", weight around 180 lbs. I don't believe he was involved in the crime.'

Whilst in Roswell, Reyos became nostalgic and, according to his trial testimony, decided to drive around part of the Eastern New Mexico University campus where he had studied two years earlier and he then stopped at a local Minit Mart, at approximately 6:30pm local time (7:30pm in Texas), bumping into an old college acquaintance named David Myer.

The two men, who were not close at college, had a chat about old times and after a short while Reyos suggested they continue their conversation over some beers. The men bought some beers and went to Myer's apartment where they stayed, according to Myer in his trial testimony, for "about an hour or an hour and a half." Reyos left Myer's apartment no earlier than 7:30pm local time, which was 8:30pm in Texas, and realistically it would have been after 8pm local time (9pm in Texas). This is because the two men had to meet and then travel to Myer's apartment. Reyos maintains he met his old friend at approximately 6:30pm at the store but unfortunately did not have a receipt for the purchase of the beer. Perhaps Myer bought the beer and discarded the receipt if he was given one. If they only met a 6:30pm, which seems plausible, then Reyos must have left no earlier than 7:30pm local time (8:30pm in Texas) and possibly as late as 8pm local time (9pm in Texas).

Myer could not be sure about the date when first asked by Reyos' defense team a year and a half after the murder. He knew it was a day shortly before Christmas, between December 19 and 23, and thought it was December 21 but he could not be certain. He was sure it was not Christmas Eve. However, he knew that Reyos had his truck with him which meant it had to be after Reyos secured the release of the truck from the bondsman, which had only taken place on December 21. It could not have been December 22 because that evening Reyos was in jail having been arrested for public intoxication. On the evening of December 23 he was in Albuquerque. Therefore Reyos must certainly have been with Myer on December 21, at precisely the same time that Father Ryan was being murdered, 200 miles away (as will soon be demonstrated).

Myer had no reason to lie because the two men were not close friends. He could not be accurate about the date because the amount of time which had passed since that December evening in 1981 and when he was first contacted to give his account of that evening, in 1983. Yet if he had been intending to lie, because Reyos had asked him to do so, he would surely have made sure he gave the date which Reyos had instructed him to.

Reyos is frustrated by the fact that Myer was not contacted by the police until a year after the murder. In the days after the murder, when first suspected of being the killer, Reyos had told the police he was in Roswell. Had the police taken a statement at that time the date would have been fresh in Myer's mind. Reyos' lawyers had struggled to locate Myer in advance of the trial, and only succeeded in doing so two months before the trial began, because Myer had got married and moved to Texas.

Despite Myer's uncertainty about the date the petrol receipts and other receipts (in total there were ten receipts) confirm Reyos was in the area on the evening of December 21 and they show that he could not therefore have been 200 miles away in Odessa or indeed anywhere in Texas.

After leaving Myer's apartment Reyos claims he drove to Bottomless Lakes State Park, less than 15 miles from Roswell, and continued to drink by himself.

Reyos cannot prove his whereabouts for much of the period between leaving Myer's apartment and midnight because of the lack of receipts for that period but he claims to have been in Tatum, New Mexico at between 9pm and 10pm and he bought gas at a Chevron station during this time, characteristically keeping his receipt which unfortunately did not have the time printed upon it, although the date is clearly stated as December 21.

A cast iron alibi has been further provided by the police who caught him speeding at 11:15pm local time (it was at this time

12:15am the following day in Texas), only fifteen miles west of Roswell, driving east towards Roswell. The state trooper who issued the ticket noticed nothing odd about Reyos' appearance, such as cuts, bruises, or bloodstained clothing. Similarly there was nothing about his demeanor which was at all suspicious other than that he had been drinking and speeding. The speeding ticket confirms he was nearly 215 miles from the scene of the murder, 15 miles to the west of Roswell, just hours after the crime.

Reyos was drunk and soon after receiving the ticket he actually crashed his vehicle into a ditch, such was his inability to drive due to his drunken state. He spun his tires until the tread had worn away on one of them and it later became flat. A passing motorist tried to assist and, realizing Reyos was drunk, drove his truck with Reyos in the passenger seat to Sambo's restaurant in Roswell where Reyos called for a truck to come and tow away his own truck. His truck was towed away at 3am local time (4am in Texas) in Reyos' presence, and taken to a Mobil station for repair.

After the repair, Reyos claims he drove back to Myer's apartment and slept outside in the truck. Myer was unaware of this but testified at trial that Reyos could have been outside his house without his knowledge and that he himself might not have been at home by that time because he often stayed out at night.

It was now the morning of December 22 and, with his tire repaired, Reyos continued to drive north, calling at an Allsup's Convenience Store, to buy beer, drinking as he drove. At a distance of around 30 miles outside of Roswell he again got a flat tire and had to have his truck towed back to the Mobil station at Roswell. This was confirmed by a receipt showing the purchase of a new tire and towing charges. The owner of the Mobil station that carried out the work also confirmed Reyos' story and told the court that Reyos was with him during the afternoon until after 6pm because the tire could not be replaced until that time due to a heavy workload. Soon afterwards Reyos was arrested for public intoxication and spent the night in Roswell jail. Upon his release, on the morning of December 23, he traveled to see his family at Dulce, near Albuquerque and stayed the night at Albuquerque.

His movements therefore on December 21 until December 23 are thus well established. Compelling evidence in the form of an alibi has left campaigners certain that a travesty of justice took place in Texas on June 10, 1983.

According to Doctor R Cohen, Ryan had been killed "more than likely" between twelve and eighteen hours before his examination of the body which had taken place at around noon, placing death between 6pm and midnight. However, Father Ryan checked into the motel at between 7:30pm and 8pm and we have already learnt that the man in the next room heard nothing all night despite the crime having been described by police officers as "an out and out fight" and the crime scene as having had what must have been "like almost a wrestling match" having taken place. That next door room was occupied from 9pm onwards by George Cooper, who stayed awake for much of the night, watching television until the early hours of the morning before sleeping. Of course, Father Ryan could have consented to having his hands tied behind his back, as part of a sex game, but there would have still been a lot of noise created during the attack. Therefore death is most likely to have taken place before 9pm but after around 7:30pm to 8pm. Given the number of cigarette butts in the room it is likely Father Ryan must have spent at least half an hour alive, in order to smoke those cigarettes (if indeed Reyos, a non smoker, was responsible). According to Reyos Father Ryan was not a heavy smoker. There is therefore a narrow window of opportunity during which the crime could have been committed and during most, if not all, of that narrow time period Reyos was with David Myer in Roswell.

I will outline a number of different scenarios to determine how likely it is that Reyos could have committed the murder. For each of the following scenarios it is assumed Father Ryan's killer must have been present for half an hour (in order to drink with Father Ryan, sexually assault him, kill him and cause the damage to the room before leaving). Each scenario is dependent upon the undisputed fact of Reyos being 15 miles west of Roswell at 11:15pm (local time), which was 12:15pm in Texas. Therefore the distance to travel was 415 miles.

If Reyos left Myer's apartment at 8pm (local time) he would have had to travel an average speed of 151 miles per hour to Odessa and back to New Mexico. This scenario is also reliant upon the murder taking place when George Cooper was in the next room, with

Cooper hearing nothing. There is no possibility that Reyos committed the murder if he left Myer's apartment at 8pm.

If he left Myer's apartment at 7:30pm he would have had to travel an average speed of 128 miles per hour to Odessa and back to New Mexico. This scenario would also be reliant upon Cooper being present but hearing nothing.

If Reyos left Myer's apartment at 7pm he would have had to travel at an average speed of 111 miles per hour for each journey and he would have also arrived at the motel after Cooper had checked in.

If Reyos left Myer's apartment at 6:30pm he would have had to travel at an average speed of 98 miles per hour for each journey. Again he would also have arrived at the motel when Cooper was present in the next room. This scenario also gives little time for Reyos to have been with Myer, whereas Myer felt sure that Reyos was with him for between an hour and an hour and a half.

Although Reyos claims he met Myer at 6:30pm, what if the men met earlier? Myer was uncertain of the time but was sure, according to his trial testimony, that "It was evening time, about dusk." On December 21 the sun sets in Roswell at 4:54pm. Civil dusk (where most objects are still distinguishable but some stars become visible) begins at 5:22pm. Playing Devil's Advocate let us consider that Reyos met Myer an hour earlier than he stated, at around 5:30pm. For this scenario to have occurred Reyos must have dropped off the hitchhiker at Roswell bus station at 5pm and then driven almost straight to the minit mart where he met Myer. The two would have chatted for a few minutes, bought beer and traveled to Myer's apartment, arriving around 5:40pm. If Reyos spent only half an hour at Myer's apartment (much less than Myer's recollection) then he could theoretically have left Roswell at around 6:15pm. In this scenario he would have had to travel an average speed of 92 miles per hour to Odessa and back if the murder was committed at a time when Cooper was in the next room. In order to have committed the murder prior to Cooper's arrival, Reyos would have needed to drive an average speed of 160 miles per hour to Odessa, kill Father Ryan, and drive back at an average speed of 66 miles per hour. Whilst the return journey speed is plausible, the journey speed to Odessa is physically impossible.

Even if we consider Reyos leaving Roswell at 6pm, and he could not possibly have left any earlier, the journey to Odessa would have been 133 miles per hour in order to commit the murder before Cooper checked in. To have committed the murder whilst Cooper was present Reyos would have had to travel an average speed of 87 miles per hour to and from Odessa. Whilst this is not impossible it is stretching credibility to suggest it was what happened and completely contradicts Myer's testimony.

The fact Reyos was driving so badly that he drove into a ditch shortly after being given a speeding ticket at 11:15pm, suggests he did not drive very far for at least a small amount of time prior to crashing. He was barely capable of driving at all. Also, given that Reyos had to fill up with gas twice on his way to Roswell earlier in the day, he would have needed to stop for gas multiple times to travel the 415 miles to Odessa and back, if indeed he was the killer, adding to the journey time.

It is impossible that the murder could have taken place after midnight, if Reyos was responsible, because he was drunk and without a vehicle so he had no way of getting to Odessa following his crash into the roadside ditch.

Reyos believes his innocence can be proven by this alibi. 'I believe the trial evidence – my alibi – speaks for itself.', he says, adding:

> 'I COULD NOT have killed Father Ryan. My alibi places me 200 miles away from the scene of the crime. It is a "provable account" of my whereabouts during the commission of the crime which would make it "impossible or impracticable" to place me at the murder scene!'

The collection and retention of receipts was very ordinary for Reyos and not what would later be described as some convenient attempt to construct an alibi. In fact he had, as the reader may recall, produced them to the police five days after the murder when he had been considered a suspect and doubtless he retained them in case he was questioned about the crime again. It is not too unusual for anyone to keep receipts for days on end. In fact my wallet often has receipts which can sometimes be a month or older in date.

Although he had a somewhat chaotic life as a result of his alcoholic lifestyle Reyos is a creature of habit. When released on parole in December 2003 he began to live a very ordered life. Even the tuna tins in his room were all facing the same way, when he was visited by a journalist in 2005. Perhaps this is partly the consequence of his prison life and therefore may not have existed prior to his conviction. Everything about a Texas prisoner's life in incarceration is designed to take away their original personality, from their uniform to their daily activities and other aspects of their regime which some former inmates have described as the 'prison system's depersonalization process.' In Britain we call it the process of institutionalization. Nonetheless his collection of documentation is something that was an element of his personality back in 1981 and so his possession of the receipts when arrested in 1982 was not out of character and certainly not suspicious.

Even if Reyos could drive to Odessa, from Roswell, in the very limited time available, how could he have also moved his alleged victim's car during this period of time? Father Ryan's car was found abandoned outside the Moose Lodge in Hobbs, approximately 70 miles from the crime scene, on Christmas Eve, having been stolen from the Sand and Sage Motel after the crime. It would be too incredible to believe that Father Ryan was murdered, and his car stolen, in two completely unrelated events, with two unconnected individuals. Therefore his killer must have stolen the vehicle, and then abandoned it three days later. Unless Reyos had an accomplice, and there has never been any evidence to suggest he had one, he could not have traveled from Roswell to Odessa, commit the murder, drive the truck somewhere with the intention of taking it to Hobbs at a later date, somehow get back to Odessa and then travel to Roswell in such a short period of time. It is absolutely impossible.

I do believe that it is very possible that Father Ryan's killer had an accomplice, if only for the movement of Father Ryan's vehicle, but the alibi demonstrates neither of those men could have been James Harry Reyos.

We only know the vehicle was abandoned at the Moose Lodge on Christmas Eve. Where it was before then is unknown. So where was Reyos on Christmas Eve? Could he have been in Hobbs? The answer is certainly, no. Having been arrested on December 22 for public intoxication he was released on December 23 and then traveled to his family, staying at Albuquerque and not leaving until Christmas Day. He then drove to Roswell where he spent the night, before returning to Denver City on 26 December, arriving at around 10am or 11am and being spoken to by the police later that day. 'From approximately 11:30 a.m. Monday, December 21, 1981 to Saturday, December 26, 1981 I WAS IN THE STATE OF NEW MEXICO.', Reyos writes.

At Reyos' trial a witness named Olivia Gonzales testified that she had seen Reyos driving Father Ryan's vehicle the day after the murder. If true this would point to his guilt. However, Reyos was in Roswell that day and could not have been the man Gonzales had seen. If Gonzales was correct that someone was driving Father Ryan's car on the day after the murder, then this would prove that someone other than Reyos was in possession of the stolen vehicle. That point alone proves he did not steal the vehicle from the Sand and Sage motel and that some other individual was involved in the murder.

Forensic Evidence

The French pioneering forensic scientist Dr Edmond Locard, who lived from 1877 to 1966, famously wrote, 'Every contact leaves a trace'. How true these words, which are known as 'Locard's exchange principle', are. With large numbers of fingerprints, blood, semen, hairs and saliva at the crime scene the killer of Father Patrick Ryan certainly left his trace, so who does that forensic evidence suggest was the perpetrator?

The forensic evidence points to an unknown individual having been the killer (or possibly two or more individuals being responsible). Reyos' fingerprints did not match any of the bloodstained fingerprints at the crime scene and hairs and saliva found around the body came from some unidentified person or persons. The killer(s) was/were careless, causing so much destruction to the furniture in the room and leaving a trail of forensic evidence in the form of hairs, semen, saliva and prints, that if Reyos was guilty there should have been some trace of him.

An FBI lab report dated April 27, 1983 stated: 'The five latent fingerprints and the two latent impressions are not the fingerprints or palm prints of Reyos.'

At trial the report was corroborated by Odessa Police (taken verbatim from the trial transcripts: Volume 3, page 10):

> Q. [Defense Attorney] Did you have the opportunity to obtain Mr. Reyos' fingerprints?
> A. [Odessa Police Detective] Yes, Sir, I did.
> Q. Did you compare these fingerprints to any prints found in the room?
> A. Yes, Sir, I did.
> Q. Did you find any prints in the room that matched his fingerprints?
> A. There was none that we could positively say were his.
> Q. So you didn't find any fingerprints that you could say were his in the room where the body was found?
> A. No, sir.

So who did those fingerprints belong to? Later in the trial there was further testimony regarding fingerprints (trial transcripts, volume 5, pages 57 and 58):

> Q. [Defense Attorney] All right. Now, fingerprints were taken in the room. Is that correct?
> A. [Odessa Homicide Detective] Yes, sir.
> Q. Fingerprints – they tried to get fingerprints off the beer cans also, didn't they?
> A. Yes, sir, that's correct.
> Q. Those proved negative, as far as James is concerned, didn't they?
> A. That's correct.

The Texas Department of Public Safety Crime Lab in Midland wrote, on May 30, 1983, 'None of the numerous hairs from the scene previously examined resembled head or pubic hair from the suspect (Reyos).'

Again, this report was not disputed at trial by the police (taken verbatim from the transcripts: volume 5, page 65):

> Q. [Defense Attorney] Okay. Now, at a future date on May 5th, 1983, did you receive some blood, hair and saliva samples from the Ector County District's Office which had been taken from Mr. James Harry Reyos here?
> A. [Chemist, Texas DPS] Yes, I did.
> Q. Okay. And did you compare these hair samples with the hair samples found in the bedding in the motel room to determine whether or not they matched?
> A. I made such a comparison, yes.
> Q. Did the hair samples found in the bedding that didn't match the deceased, did they match the hair given to you from James Harry Reyos?
> A. No, they didn't.

It is also worth repeating the fact that in the days after the murder Reyos had no bruises, scratches or cuts consistent with the violent struggle that he supposedly had with his alleged victim.

It is worth repeating that although there were a large number of beer cans and discarded cigarette butts at the crime scene, Reyos did not smoke.

Whilst absence of evidence is not evidence of absence, the fact that none of the blood, semen, hairs or fingerprints at the crime scene matched Reyos seems to strongly suggest that the culprit was another man. For such a violent crime it seems incredible that Reyos did not leave any trace of him having been present at the scene, and it entirely works against Locard's exchange principle that 'every contact leaves a trace.' The forensic evidence would seem to suggest Reyos was never in the Sand and Sage Motel yet some unidentified individual was present at the time that Father Ryan lost his life. Who was that individual?

Unfortunately all of the forensic evidence was destroyed in 1993, in breach of the State police's own policies, meaning that it cannot now be subjected to modern forensic examination to identify the true culprit or culprits. The police had failed to mention, to Reyos or his lawyers, their intention to destroy the evidence and the discovery that the evidence had been destroyed only came about when Reyos' lawyer made a request to compare fingerprints with those of another possible suspect, who will be discussed in a later chapter.

The Conviction

All of the evidence, taking a cold examination of the facts, indicates that some unknown individual committed a barbaric murder whilst James Harry Reyos was approximately 200 miles away from the scene of the crime. If we are to put the confession, which it can be argued was unreliable, to one side there is no physical evidence to link Reyos to the crime scene or the crime. There were no witnesses and there was only a possible motive. The prosecution's case was tenuous.

However, the evidence (or lack of it) was sufficient in the opinion of the twelve members of the jury. On June 10, 1983, at the conclusion of the four day trial, the jury retired to consider its verdict. After deliberating for seven and a half hours they filed back into the court room, late in the night, and the announcement was made that the jury were in agreement over their verdict. James Harry Reyos was, the judge said when reading out the jury's verdict, guilty of murder.

Upon hearing the Guilty verdict, Reyos thanked his defense team. It is typical of Reyos that even in one of the most difficult situations a person can face, being labeled a murderer and knowing he might die in prison or be released as a very old man, one of his first thoughts was to thank his lawyers for their efforts. It was only as he was taken away that the reality of the situation hit him.

In November 2013 I asked Reyos to describe to me in detail how he felt upon being convicted. We had discussed it previously but I wanted to have a more detailed written account for the purposes of this book.

> 'Prior to trial I always thought I would be found "Not Guilty" because of the substantial, overwhelming and credible evidence proving my actual innocence. My trial attorneys also felt very confident that I would be found Not Guilty. My family felt the same way too. However, that is not how it turned out. I felt in my heart that the criminal justice system failed me. I have always felt that our system of justice here in the United States is fair. It was not a very good feeling when I first heard the verdict. Frankly, I was shocked, disappointed and a little bitter.

Once the trial was over that Friday afternoon, the jury immediately went into deliberation. They deliberated for approximately 7.5 hours, rendering a verdict at 10:30p.m. At one point I asked my attorney why it was taking so long for them to reach a verdict. He told me that usually the longer it takes the better, because one or more jurors are holding out; that they are not sure of a guilty verdict. Of course, I felt a little more confident that they will come back with a Not Guilty verdict. Not so. When I heard the judge read the jury's decision, I shook my head, buried my head in my hands and weep a little. I just couldn't believe they reached that verdict. I thought to myself, what evidence did they rely on when all the other evidence proves my ACTUAL innocence.'

For Reyos not only was the verdict decided by the jury, but so was his sentence. The jury believed that Reyos should be sent to prison for 38 years and this choice of sentence has raised some questions.

It has been suggested that the jury may have had doubts about his guilt because if they were convinced of his guilt why did they not sentence him to life without the prospect of parole, instead sentencing him only to 38 years? It was, it has been argued, as if they wanted to give him a chance of experiencing freedom once again but that they wanted to ensure someone was held to account.

With the passing of the verdict, and sentence, so began one of America's most controversial criminal convictions and in my opinion one of the country's most serious and damning miscarriages of justice.

Why did they convict when there were so many grounds for doubt? Reyos told me his theory, that he was the victim of discrimination.

It is not surprising Reyos believes there was prejudice against him. One of the senior detectives investigating the murder to this day refers to Reyos as the "Indian boy." Indeed during a documentary about the case the detective only referred to Reyos as the "Indian boy."

The police were clearly influenced by Reyos' race, but what about the jury? Remember that a member of the jury remarked on how Reyos' "characteristics", along with his confession, were a factor in their decision. These "characteristics" can only be his race and his sexuality. Reyos once wrote to me about the discrimination he feels he was victim of, on account of race, sexuality and his accusations against Father Ryan:

> 'I do believe that my ethnic background played a role during my 1983 trial. The city where the trial was held (Odessa, Texas, Ector County) is a so-called redneck town. The jury was composed of mostly whites. I do believe that there was prejudice toward me because of my ethnic background, my personal lifestyle, who the victim was (a prominent Catholic priest), and the seriousness and nature of the crime. Back in the early 1980s, you did not hear too much of Catholic priest sexually abusing young boys and young men; today, it's more prevalent. I believe that the testimony by me -- and two other young men -- about Father Ryan's background, hurt me in the eyes of the jury. They (the jury) did not want to fully fathom the fact that "a priest" could be capable of committing such sexual offenses. Today, as you know, the Catholic church is struggling with the many, many stories of sexual abuse by priests. I believe that Father Ryan's own aggressive sexual behavior lead to his demise.'

Reyos adds that that the jury refused to believe his claims regarding Father Ryan's sexual predatory nature:

> 'Back in the 1980s you did not hear too much of Catholic priests sexually abusing young boys and young men. Today it's more prevalent. I believe that the testimony by me – and two other young men – about Father Ryan's background hurt me in the eyes of the jury. They (the jury) did not want to fully fathom the fact that "a priest" could be capable of committing such sexual offences.'

There is, however, strong evidence that Father Ryan was a serial sexual offender and that he was one of many such offenders who were known as 'program priests'.

"The Program Priests"

"Jesus paid the price for our sinfulness by his death on the cross. We, as his disciples, we get a share in that. And we're getting a big share right now."

These are the words of Bishop Yanta speaking to the Dallas Morning News about the sex abuse scandal in the Amarillo Diocese, the diocese Father Ryan began to serve in 1979. During the trial of James Harry Reyos it emerged from three individuals, one of whom was Reyos and the other two being individuals who had never met Reyos, that Father Ryan was a sexual predator with a fondness for young men. In 1983, when Reyos stood trial, the presence of sexually active homosexuals within the church was considered by the outside world to be a myth, and that those who claimed to be victims were troubled individuals who were fabricating their stories.

The abuse by some priests of young men has been highlighted in recent decades and has caused many scandals in the Roman Catholic Church. It is now an accepted fact that some priests in Texas, and across the United States and in other countries, were committing sexual acts against men and boys, and there is overwhelming evidence that a retreat to try and treat priests committing sexual acts and offences was failing and that it directly channeled sexual predators into the Diocese where Father Patrick Ryan served.

The Jemez Springs retreat was the brainchild of Father Gerald Fitzgerald who wanted to create a safe community whose mission was to help those priests who were struggling with alcohol and drug addictions. The idea came to him when a beggar turned up on his doorstep seeking help only to then inform the priest that he too had once been a member of the clergy who had fallen on hard times. Feeling that he needed to offer a helping hand to those priests in need, Fitzgerald appealed for people to provide a location for a retreat and his only reply was Archbishop Edwin Byrne of Santa Fe who assisted him in buying land in Jemez Springs, New Mexico, where he founded 'The congregation of the Servants of the Paraclete' in Jemez Springs.

The retreat grew and eventually began accepting priests who were struggling with celibacy and were actually committing sexual offences. The priests underwent a 'program' of treatment, based largely on intense prayer, and its conceived success and the demand for the 'program' increased, resulting in 23 centers being opened across the country, with additional half way houses being set up to help priests re-enter the community. One of these halfway houses was in Albuquerque.

Father Fitzgerald refused to allow any priest who had been at the retreat to return to active life as a priest, although some bishops ignored him. It was his belief that those priests guilty of sexual offences could not be cured. His views on the matter are abundantly clear in a letter to Archbishop Byrne in 1957:

> 'May I beg Your Excellency to concur and approve of what I consider a very vital decision on our part – that we will not offer hospitality to men who have seduced or attempted to seduce little boys or girls. These men Your Excellency are devils and the wrath of God is upon them and if I were a bishop I would tremble when I failed to report them to Rome for involuntary laicization. ... It is for this class of rattlesnake I have always wished the island retreat – but even an island is too good for these vipers of whom the Gentle master said – it were better they had not been born – this is an indirect way of saying damned, is it not? When I see the Holy Father I am going to speak of this class to his Holiness.'

In a 1964 letter to Bishop Joseph Durick of Nashville, Tennessee, Fitzgerald expressed "growing concern" about the rising number of priests who were having sexual relations with men. He wrote:

> 'May I take this occasion to bring to your attention what is a growing concern to many of us here in the States. When I was ordained, forty three years ago, homosexuality was a practically unknown rarity. Today it is rampant among men. And whereas seventeen years ago eight out of ten problems here [the Paraclete facility, Via Coeli] would represent the alcoholic, now in the last year or so our admission ratio would be approximately 5-2-3: five being alcoholic, two would be what we call "heart cases" (natural affection towards women) and three representing aberrations involving homosexuality. More

alarming still is that among these of the 3 out of 10 class, 2 out of 3 have been young priests.'

After meeting Pope Paul VI in August 1963, Fitzgerald began to believe that priests could return to their duties but only with careful supervision. He had discussed, with the newly elected Pope, his work and the problems he frequently encountered within the priesthood. After his meeting with the Pope he wrote:

> "Personally I am not sanguine of the return of priests to active duty who have been addicted to abnormal practices, especially sins with the young. However, the needs of the church must be taken into consideration and an activation of priests who have seemingly recovered in this field may be considered but is only recommended where careful guidance and supervision is possible. Where there is indication of incorrigibility, because of the tremendous scandal given, I would most earnestly recommend total laicization."

Until his death in 1967, Fitzgerald was opposed to having to take in priests who molested minors, on account of them being 'too dangerous'. His hopes to create an island retreat, to completely isolate priests responsible for serious sexual offences, had to be abandoned due to a lack of funds and a lack of support from Archbishop Byrne's successor. For the rest of his life Fitzgerald continued to make recommendations that priests on the program should not be allowed to return to active service within communities. However, following his death these recommendations ceased and 'program priests' began to return to serving the community in larger numbers.

Between 1985 and 2008, 365 priests are recorded as having stayed at the retreat for sex offences and of these 22 (6%) are known to have relapsed. However, given that it has been proven many sex offences have gone unreported or were not discovered until years, and sometimes decades later, then it is likely more than the official 6% of those who went to Jemez Springs went on to commit further acts. And this does not include data from before 1985. The center had been treating sex offenders long before that year. There were also, of course, other centers in addition to that at Jemez Springs.

One of the key recipients of these 'program priests' was the Amarillo Diocese, which was where Father Patrick Ryan was first recorded as having served during his time in the USA. The Bishop who appointed Ryan, Bishop Leroy Matthiesen, could not (he claimed) recall where he found Father Ryan, or where Father Ryan had served prior to arriving at Amarillo, which is remarkable given his otherwise sharp memory. I believe he found Father Ryan at Jemez Springs, where the Bishop obtained a large proportion of the priests for the diocese, Bishop Matthiesen was doubtless aware of Father Ryan's sexual behavior. Why else would he have been such a strong supporter of Reyos right up until his death?

Bishop Matthiesen, his predecessor, and his successor Bishop Yanta, did indeed cumulatively acquire many priests from Jemez Springs, and appointed them within the Diocese. In fact when, in 2004, the 'program priests' were banned from serving, the Amarillo Diocese lost one quarter of all its priests. Bishop Matthiesen later remarked that he had regretted taking on six priests he met between 1988 and 1995 but otherwise he was proud to have given abusers a second chance. "I personally have not regretted taking them.", Bishop Matthiesen was quoted as saying.

The priests also were required to meet monthly with the Bishop, return to Jemez Springs every six months, attend a support group headed by a psychologist and receive individual counseling, Bishop Matthiesen said.

It was not until soon before 2004, Bishop Matthiesen said, that he learned some priests were not the first-time sex offenders that they purported to be when he agreed to hire them. "I was too focused on the needs of the priests rather than thinking about the victims.", he said.

The Bishop appointed child molesters even when criminal charges had been brought against them. For example, he appointed Father Salazar-Jimenez in 1991 whilst the priest was on parole for child molestation, having spent time in prison for molesting two teenage boys.

He claims to have had a zero tolerance attitude towards priests who molested children, but this is evident only in the case of one foreign priest who had been accused of molesting altar boys, who he told to "get out by sundown", according to an interview to the Dallas Morning News on 19 January 2004.

Bishop Matthiesen said he hid the truth about Father Salazar-Jimenez and the other priests hired from treatment programs as part of an after-care program intended to keep them from committing new offenses.

Bishop Matthiesen had been aware of the Jemez Springs retreat from the very beginning of its association with sex offender priests and although he admitted to appointing priests from the retreat from 1988, he had been visiting Jemez Springs from 1982, if not earlier, and may well have had connections with the Center before that year. He also hired a priest from another Center, the St Luke Institute in Suitland, for the treatment of priests who were sexual offenders.

Bishop Yanta admitted, in early 2004, that there had been 17 priests in the Amarillo Diocese where there was reasonable cause to believe that the priests were sexual offenders, who had abused 41 minors over a period of 52 years. The admission followed a study by the Office of Protection of Children and Youth of the U.S. Conference of Catholic Bishops and the John Jay College of Criminal Science. It is likely there were additional priests who abused other minors, but it is also highly likely there were priests who only abused young adults. The figure is likely to be higher than only 17.

According to Yanta's letter, of the 17 priests 9 were dead and the remaining 8 had been removed from active service. Who were these 17 priests? Could Father Ryan have been one? Unfortunately the church refuses to name those who have been identified as sexual offenders.

Yanta's letter continued:

> 'Particularly, I express an apology to those who have been abused by a deacon, priest or leader of the church. While we cannot change the past, I do want to continue to reach out to those who have been hurt and victimized, and offer my personal prayers and the support of our local church. I pray for victims, both in our diocese and throughout our country, daily and hope that they will know and experience the healing that God alone can give.'

Although he apologized to the victims, Bishop Yanta refused to apologize for the church's secrecy, believing that bishops had a right to protect the reputation of priests. "The communication of the truth is not a universal right," he said in an interview to the Dallas Morning News on January 19, 2004. It is a remarkable statement because surely truth and justice are a very basic, universal, human right.

Prison

Convicted of murder and sentenced to 38 years imprisonment, Reyos now faced the prospect of dying behind bars or returning to society as an old man. After thanking his legal team he was taken to the cells to await processing and transportation to the Coffield Unit in Tennessee Colony, Texas.

The journey was made by a prison (chain) bus and was, he recently recalled, 'a very long ride on the chain bus, about six hours.' During this journey he sat, wondering how long he might be locked up for a crime he did not commit, unable to comprehend how this conviction had happened.

Coffield Unit is a large prison and at the time of Reyos' arrival he believes there were approximately 4200 inmates. I asked him to write about his first night in prison and I present here his unaltered words, because it is Reyos' words that provide the best possible account of what this experience was like:

'I remember getting off the chain bus, walking down a long, long hallway to the Majors Office to be assigned a cell. After being assigned a cell, we were escorted to the laundry to get our bed linens and prison uniforms (what are called "whites"). We were then escorted down the same long hallway to our cellblocks. We arrived at Coffield around 11:00p.m. Everybody was already racked up (put in their cells). I carried my linens, prison uniforms, and a small paper bag with a few letters from my family and attorneys.

'I was led up to 3-Row (3rd floor) to my now new living quarters. The Boss (prison guard) opened the cell door for me and I stepped in. The cell was very dark; I tried to turn on the light but there was no light bulb in the socket, so I had to find my way around in the cell. I threw my stuff on the top bunk (I did not have a cellmate for almost a year). I made my bunk and then sat down on it, staring at the dark wall, thinking about "what is this place like?" and "how long will I be here?" I could hear radios playing, inmates talking. Several inmates yelled at me asking who I was, what my crime was, how much time did I get? I really did not feel like talking to anybody, so all I said was "I will talk to you tomorrow."

'I laid down and could not believe that I was now in a state prison. It was a very lonely feeling for me that night, knowing that the judicial system failed me, and that I would be a very long distance from my family. I thought about my Dad who I last saw at the county jail after the trial was over. Seeing him in that visiting room with his walking cane talking to me brought tears to my eyes while I laid on my bunk at Coffield. One thing I will never forget is his last words of advice to me at Ector County jail, when he told me: "Son, always be strong. Don't ever give up." The next day when I woke up at Coffield, I got a piece of paper and pencil and wrote those words down and stuck it up on the wall next to my bunk so that I could read them every morning when I got up, and every night when I went to bed.'

The Fight for Justice Begins

Reyos' first attempt to overturn his conviction was made in November 1984 when his attorney, John Cliff, challenged whether a recanted confession should have been sufficient evidence to support the guilty verdict. The appeal was on a point of law and did not ask whether the recanted confession should have been admissible as evidence. It was ruled that the confession was sufficient and that Reyos' conviction was justifiable. On the face of it, it appeared Reyos had no hope of release without serving his sentence.

Yet Reyos has never given up hope and has kept his father's words at the forefront of his mind. Given the alibi, the lack of forensic evidence and arguments suggesting the confession was unreliable Reyos has campaigned vigorously and in the course of his battle he has gained a large amount of supporters. His cause is backed by politicians, journalists and large numbers of the public. His trial defense attorney said in December 2003, following his appointment as District Attorney for Ector County, 'I will go to my grave thinking Harry is innocent. That's John W. Smith the lawyer speaking. As D.A. I can't take a position.'

Smith's colleague, John W. Cliffe, who was the second defense attorney at trial, has added his support in a letter to Reyos in February 2003, 'As I've said many times, to you and others, your conviction is the only one in my entire career that I am absolutely convinced was wrong.'

Even the prosecuting attorney, who led the prosecution at Reyos' 1984 appeal, has since come to accept that a miscarriage of justice has taken place. In preparation for the appeal Dennis Cadra did not familiarize himself with the evidence and the full facts of the case, dealing simply with points of law, which raises worrying questions about the system that allows an appeal to be argued against by prosecutors who do not fully understand the case. The people should be represented by a team who know the full facts and understand the case when a man's liberty is at stake. He later claimed he had seen 'superficial flaws' in the prosecution's case, largely on the basis of the alibi, but did not have sufficient time to fully examine the case because the brief needed to be completed in a short period of time and did not require the close examination of all of the case papers.

Cadra had been satisfied that the confession alone was enough to show Reyos was a murderer, and presented the prosecution's argument, resulting in Reyos' appeal being dismissed.

However, seven years later, when asked by the Ector County District clerk whether he still needed trial transcripts, including those of the Reyos trial, Cadra decided to look at them. He read through the seven volumes of transcripts over a Sunday night and into the Monday morning, not even going home. He was astounded by what he saw. On December 31, 1991 Cadra wrote an 8-page letter to the then Governor of Texas, Ann Richards. I have a copy of that letter, which summarizes all of the facts and concentrates on the issue of Reyos' alibi. However, it also includes some information relating to interviews he had with other prosecutors involved in the case and also Jerry Smith, the lead police investigator in Father Ryan's murder. With regards to Jerry Smith, Cadra wrote that Smith was not certain of Reyos' guilt. Cadra and Smith knew one another very well and often drank together.

The research Cadra undertook led him to make an astonishing claim:

> 'Despite my 16 years as a prosecutor, I came to the firm conclusion that it was physically impossible for Mr. Reyos to have committed the crime for which he has been in a Texas penitentiary for almost eight years.'

His letter ended with the following words:

> 'Thank you in advance for your attention and please forgive me for this egregiously long letter. I know the demands on your time are overwhelming, but I feel I would be remiss in my duties as a citizen and as a public official if I did not pass this information on to you and the Board of Pardons and Paroles before I leave this office. Quite frankly, I am somewhat ashamed that I did not fully investigate this matter when I first developed doubts about Mr Reyos guilt.'

Up until his death Dennis Cadra continued to campaign for Reyos and in 2003 he spoke on TV's *American Justice,* saying, "Mr Reyos couldn't have, couldn't have committed the murder."

As a result of Cadra's assessment of the evidence the Governor asked, in 1992, for a review of the case and the Texas Civil Rights Project filed a writ of habeas corpus petition at the Court of Criminal Appeal. Cadra's opinion was dismissed by J. Anthony Foster, who was one of the two district attorneys who prosecuted Reyos. Foster told the Board that they should not be swayed by "Monday morning quarterbacks."

The appeal was ultimately rejected, without any formal hearing taking place and with no written judgment. Reyos learnt of his fate when the court sent their ruling on a postcard. Jim Harrington, Director of the Texas Civil Rights Project felt sure that racism played a role in Reyos' original conviction and the decision not to allow his appeal. He believes the justice system in the USA as a whole is plagued by institutional racism, although this is disputed by prosecutors.

Ector County Judge Jay Gibson argued that the appeal was rejected because there was no new evidence in the case. Although serious doubts were cast on the evidence to convict, especially regarding the fact Reyos was 200 miles away on the night of the murder, the jury had been made aware of that fact at trial and had still concluded Reyos was guilty. As a result, Gibson argued, his hands were tied. "The law bound me to go with what the jury said.", Gibson later said.

It was Reyos' last legal chance of appeal and so as a result his only course to secure freedom was through the Texas Board of Pardons and Paroles and the hope was that Reyos would be granted a Full Pardon Based Upon Innocence, which would overturn his conviction, clear his name and give him complete freedom to get on with his life.

Texas is only one of nine states in the USA to have a Board of Pardons and Paroles. The duties of the Texas Board of Pardons and Paroles were set out by Article IV, Section 11, of the Texas Constitution. The Board is responsible for determining which prisoners are due to be released on parole or discretionary mandatory supervision, determining conditions of parole and mandatory supervision, determining revocation of parole and mandatory supervision and recommending the resolution of clemency matters to the Governor.

There are two ways to allow the Board of Pardons and Paroles to consider granting a full pardon on the grounds of innocence. Firstly, the prosecutor, judge and sheriff of the trial must all agree that the conviction is wrong and send a report to the Board. Secondly, the State Governor can request the Board to investigate the case and make a recommendation. In Reyos' case letters were repeatedly sent to the prosecutor, judge and sheriff but no responses were received. One of two assistant district attorneys who prosecuted Reyos, J. Anthony Foster, later stated he had no doubt about Reyos' guilt, because of the confession. It was therefore decided to concentrate efforts in persuading the Governor to intervene. If the Governor finds sufficient grounds to begin a review he or she will pass the case to the Board of Pardons and Paroles for their consideration. The Board will ask the convict to provide evidence in support of their case. The Board will then reach its decision and make a recommendation to the Governor. The Governor can then issue a Pardon or reject the case.

With this in mind Reyos and his legal team began to appeal to the sense of justice of a succession of governors, initially Ann Richards and then George W. Bush

On July 21, 1995 Reyos was released on parole, under the state's mandatory supervision law, because he had served a third of his time in prison and had behaved in an exemplary way. Recalling his release he described to me the feelings he had experienced:

> 'After 12.5 years I was happy to be out. Being on parole you are still under the jurisdiction of the state. Sure, you are free from the prison bars etc, but you are still not totally free. Being that I am ACTUALLY innocent of the crime, I would have liked to have left prison, not on parole, but via complete exoneration based upon actual innocence and via a full pardon.'

Shortly before his release he gave a media interview in which he remarked, "Being here for a crime I didn't commit, the system does not work at all. There's no such thing as justice." He added:

> "I'm going to pursue my case until the day I clear my name. I feel that the only right action yet to be taken is a full pardon. I rightfully deserve that based upon the evidence."

It was perhaps due to his anger at having the label of 'murderer' still hanging above his head that led Reyos to return to his alcoholism. After more than a decade behind bars Reyos was a damaged man. He had entered prison with difficulties. It was these difficulties that had resulted in his confession. Being locked up in a hostile prison, not knowing what his fate would be, fearing for his safety and shut away from his family and friends, only made his problems worse. Released from prison, unable to adapt to life on parole, with restricted movements, he could not cope and returned to heavy drinking. Just seven months after being freed his parole was revoked for a drink driving offence.

Once again he became inmate #359384, at the Telford Unit in New Boston. He was kept in the protective custody section for his own safety. Reyos is a vulnerable man who differed tremendously from other prisoners. He does not display a violent disposition and he is a gentle individual. However, he is convicted of a sex murder, a sex murder against a member of the clergy. This makes his crime all the more despicable in the minds of even those who have committed violent murders and consequently made Reyos a target from other inmates. Whilst in the Telford Unit he worked in the prison laundry and for some time was a teacher's assistant, which he enjoyed greatly because it gave him the opportunity to help others. When not carrying out prison work he spent considerable time reading his case papers and contacting the outside world to increase support for his cause from politicians, church organizations, the media and the public at large.

Reyos' brother gave him money to hire Adam O. Fellows and Sean Rommel, two lawyers who it was believed could greatly help his case by convincing the prosecutor, judge and sheriff of his innocence, or by persuading the Governor of Texas to send the case to the Board of Pardons and Paroles in order that he could obtain a Full Pardon Based Upon Innocence.

Whilst Reyos' lawyers made legal moves to try and overturn the conviction, Reyos once again began petitioning the series of politicians who held the position of Governor of Texas. Numerous letters were sent to George W. Bush and, later, Rick Perry. Reyos is a frequent letter writer and has written many letters to the Governors to intervene in his case and to make a recommendation to the Texas

Board of Pardons and Parole to exonerate him. I have copies of many of these letters and will detail two of them here.

During the Fall of 2000 James Harry Reyos wrote to George W. Bush, the then-Governor of Texas. Part of his letter states:

> 'Martin Luther King once said, "Injustice anywhere is a threat to justice everywhere." There exists a great injustice here in Texas – still after eighteen long years! Governor Bush, I bring to your attention my unjust plight. For eighteen long years I have been incarcerated in the Texas Department of Criminal Justice for a crime I NEVER committed. I can with all sincerity – knowing that I am telling you the honest truth! – assert that I DID NOT KILL FATHER PATRICK RYAN! I AM TOTALLY INNOCENT!'

His letter then outlined the evidence of his alibi and his increasing level of support, including that of Dennis Cadra.

Reyos' letter urged Bush to look at his case and noted how Bush had previously intervened in the case of Henry Lee Lucas and he asked that his own case be given the same attention, writing:

> 'Governor Bush, I now appeal to you at this time as the leader of Texas to ask that you intervene on my behalf – on behalf of a truly innocent man! – to help bring this 18 year injustice to an end. Please, Governor, don't give me "the deaf ear."'

Reyos' letter ended:

> 'Governor Bush, please don't allow my 18 year injustice to be a further threat to justice here in Texas. I AM TRULY INNOCENT! Justice demands nothing less than a full pardon. I was innocent yesterday! – I am innocent today! – I will be innocent in perpetuity!!!'

The letter of petition was ignored by George W. Bush who was, of course, concentrating on his presidential ambitions. It was passed to his successor, Rick Perry, who first came across it in 2001.

When Bush was elected President in 2000, Reyos began petitioning his successor, Governor Rick Perry. A number of letters were sent, with summaries of the key aspects of Reyos' defense. In one such letter, sent by Reyos on June 9, 2003, Reyos wrote:

> 'Twenty years ago tomorrow – on June 10, 1983 – I was wrongly convicted of a murder I DID NOT COMMIT. Why does a truly innocent man continue to languish in a Texas prison, despite substantial and credible evidence proving innocence? My Pardon Petition, which was filed on November 2, 2000 to the then Governor George W. Bush, should be on your desk in the process of being reviewed, with a formal decision made soon by your office.'

Reyos letter continued:

> 'I know in my heart, Governor Perry, that I AM TRULY INNOCENT of the murder of Father Patrick Ryan, a Catholic priest, from Denver city, Texas. The evidence presented at trial overwhelmingly, substantially – and credibly! – PROVED my innocence. So, PRIOR to trial, I WAS INNOCENT. Twenty years later, I AM STILL INNOCENT! Even Dennis Cadra, the former prosecuting attorney, believes I am truly innocent. ...'

Reyos' letter again ended with a plea to the Governor:

> 'Governor Perry, I am truly innocent. Please don't let me languish in Telford Unit prison any longer. I AM TRULY INNOCENT! "JUSTICE demands nothing less than a Full Pardon Based Upon Innocence.'

Reyos' letters to Perry went unanswered, as did emails and letters I, and other supporters, would later send to his office. His tough stance on crime is well known and he is a strong supporter of the death penalty. Indeed he vetoed a ban on the execution of mentally retarded prisoners. He is proud of Texas' record of the number of executions under his governorship. His tough stance has come with controversy, having refused to intervene in executions where there has been doubt about the guilt of the convict. With such a stance towards crime and punishment we knew it would be an extremely difficult task to interest Perry in the case of James Harry Reyos.

Surprisingly Father Ryan's bishop, Bishop Matthiesen, agreed to publicly support Reyos and wrote to the authorities 'I too believe he is innocent. I share the conviction that there was a miscarriage of justice.' I have a copy of a letter from Matthiesen, written to Reyos, which says:

> 'My profound hope and my prayer is that your years of unjustly incarceration will soon come to an end, and that you will be able to enjoy the freedom you lost and which you richly deserve to have restored.'

The petition was opposed, however, by other men of the cloth. Father Sean Sweeney and Rev Michael J Sheehan protested his release. The refusal of other Catholic priests to support Reyos' attempts for release came as a great disappointment. Reyos told me:

> 'It is truly sad that men of their calibre (men of God) they would protest an innocent man's release. I will say, Scott, I hold nothing against them for doing that to me. I must forgive them for what they have done, which is a mandate from my Great Spirit (to have forgiveness for those who have wronged you). I feel good in my heart that I have found forgiveness toward all those who have judged me guilty. All I can do at this time is pray to the Great Spirit that He will have mercy upon those who have judged me guilty, that He will show the mercy upon them when they stand before Him on judgment day – for they know what they did.'

Could it be that Matthiesen was such a strong supporter up until his death because he knew the crimes perpetrated by Father Ryan? The Bishop's words to Governor Perry in a letter dated June 4, 2003 are interesting:

> 'I write to urge you to grant a full pardon to JAMES HARRY REYOS who was convicted of a crime, the murder of Father Patrick Ryan, a priest working in the Diocese of Amarillo at the time I was Bishop of the Diocese, a crime which Reyos could not possibly have committed. ...'

Once again the pleas went unheard and Reyos' case was not recommended for a pardon. Reyos continued to serve his sentence, not knowing when, or if, he would ever be free again.

Reyos believes the Texas Board of Pardons and Paroles has not considered his case is in part because of an error that had been made in another case. In 1989 murderer Kenneth McDuff was released under the recommendation of the Board. There had been a serious overcrowding issue in Texas' prisons and to alleviate this many prisoners who were not considered to be a risk to the public were released and McDuff was one of those who was allowed to walk free. It was a major error, however, because he went on to kill several more young women. The Board's decision resulted in severe criticism and, Reyos believed, resulted in them becoming overcautious.

In the face of such adversity Reyos' belief in the Great Spirit, and his father's words, "Always be strong and don't ever give up hope.", have carried him through and in 2003 his hopes and prayers were answered, at least in part.

Free But Without Justice

After a further nine years in prison, in addition to the 12.5 years he had served before his parole in 1995, Reyos was again successful in being granted parole in December 2003. He had served approximately 22 years in prison and although he was again free, his murder conviction remained in place.

Released on parole Reyos initially moved to accommodation in El Paso before moving to a small apartment, owned by the Texas Corrections' Department, on Ben White Boulevard on South Austin Market Place in January 2004. The small room serves as a transitional living facility to enable newly released prisoners to adjust to life back in society.

Reyos' landlord, Carlos Patino, was immediately impressed by his new tenant and would later write to Reyos' parole officer, in a letter of support:

> 'My first impression of Mr Reyos, after meeting him for the first time, was very positive. He displayed a unique personality: respectful, kind, caring, intelligent, honest and easygoing. I have a high regard, and great respect, toward Mr Reyos. ... Mr Reyos has been a very prompt payer of his monthly rent, never having a delinquent payment. I can always count on him to have his monthly rent paid in full and, many times, paid in advance. This action is indicative of a man who is responsible, dependable, trustworthy and honest. I will always give a favorable recommendation for Mr James Harry Reyos.'

Upon his release Reyos worked hard to adjust to life. "I enjoy my limited freedom.", he later told me, "However, I am looking forward to being exonerated and pardoned so that I can have full liberty, to go anywhere I want, instead of being limited in my movements." Reyos' movements are carefully planned at weekly meetings with his parole officer, with a schedule being drawn up. He is unable to leave his home during the weekends and on public holidays and his restricted movements have made finding employment difficult. Despite being free, Reyos did not have true freedom and an electronic bracelet round his ankle helped track his movements and ensure he complied with his curfew. This would later be replaced with a bulky device fitted around his waist, with a GPS tracking system as part of the super intensive supervision program. Even leaving his apartment, to explore the interior of the apartment block, is not permitted.

'With my limited movements I really can't get out too much. I live the quiet life, which I enjoy.', he once told me but it was always apparent that he wanted greater freedom, particularly during weekends and holidays.

He was determined not to make the same mistake he had made when he was previously paroled, when he had begun drinking and had his parole revoked due to drink driving. In order to assist with this he attended meetings with Alcoholics Anonymous.

Whilst not searching for work, Reyos spent most of his time continuing with his campaign, writing petitions and letters to Government officials, meeting politicians and lawyers and contacting supporters and potential supporters with his limited internet access. It was through this means that I was first contacted by him, in November 2004.

It was in November 2004 that Reyos visited my website and sent me an email. His email read:

> 'Check out this miscarriage of justice. Prosecuting attorney, Dennis Cadra said the following: "Despite my 16 years as a prosecutor, I came to the firm conclusion that it was physically impossible for Mr. Reyos to have committed the crime and for which he has been in the Texas penitentiary for almost eight years." He wrote this to then-Governor Ann Richards, in 1992. The following is taken verbatim from "Shadows Of A Doubt: by Howard Swindle, Investigator Reporter, DALLAS MORNING NEWS (Sunday, July 4, 1993): "In the 6-inch prosecution file on the homicide of Patrick Joseph Ryan, there are autopsy reports, lab results, interview statements and leads that had taken detectives to Denver City [, TX], Plains [, TX], and Albuquerque and Hobbs, NM. Not in the file is any physical evidence to indicate that Mr. Reyos had ever been in Room 126 of the Sand and Sage Motel. Quite the contrary. An FBI lab report dated April 27, 1983, noted 'The five latent fingerprints and the two latent impressions are not the

fingerprints or palm prints of Reyos,' the FBI examiner wrote. Wrote the Texas Department of Public Safety Crime Lab in Midland on May 30, 1983, 'None of the numerous hair from the scene previously examined resembled head or pubic hair from the suspect (Reyos).' Also in the file is a report written by Detective Jerry Smith, the primary Odessa Police Department investigator, six days after the death of Father Ryan: 'At about 5:30 p.m., Det. Casey completed Reyos polygraph. Det. Casey advised that he felt like Reyos was truthful and was not involved in the homicide.'" On Wednesday, April 23, 2003, prosecuting attorney Dennis Cadra stated on TV's "American Justice": "Mr. Reyos couldn't have, couldn't have committed the murder." Why am I still being unjustly punished for this crime I DID NOT COMMIT?!!!!!! Thank you. James.'

Since that initial email we have exchanged many hundreds of emails and letters and we have spoken on the phone. Given that we live on opposite sides of the world we have never met but I feel I know him well and I know the details of his case very well. I have found Reyos to be a man who is a pleasure to know. He is an intelligent, caring, compassionate, decent human being. At no point in time has he ever displayed any signs of great anger, although frustration is sometimes apparent, or signs of a violent disposition. On the contrary, he conveys an image of a man who has no ill feelings towards others, even those who were responsible for his conviction.

I responded to that initial email, expressing some interest in the case. It was difficult not to be interested based upon Reyos' brief summary and I received the following email in return, on December 10, 2004:

'Mr Lomax: Thank you for your response. I truly appreciate your time. To fully delve into my case you can search the Internet by keying in my full name "James Harry Reyos". My case is very high-profile here in the United States, mainly in the state of Texas where I was convicted. I continue to fight this injustice because I know in my heart: I AM TRULY INNOCENT! ..... I DID NOT KILL FATHER PATRICK

RYAN!!!!! If there is a way that you can spread the word via internet please do.'

He told me that the previous day he had been interviewed by a local TV station which was making a program to be broadcast about the case to mark the 23rd anniversary of the murder and added:

> 'I currently have a Pardon Petition sitting on the desk of Texas Governor Rick Perry, awaiting a formal decision. I hope that JUSTICE will prevail, by Governor Rick Perry granting and signing the petition. JUSTICE must prevail! I wrote to INSIDE/OUTSIDE in England, an organization that supports innocent people in prison, however I never received a reply. I've also written to numerous Innocent Projects; most responding that they cannot help me because I do not live in their state. Despite all these setbacks I continue to fight for JUSTICE on my own. Thank you for your time. I look forward to hearing from you, via Email or snail mail. Please have a nice day. James.'

During this period I was busy searching for a job having recently graduated from university. I was also heavily involved in the campaign to free Barry George, as well as the campaigns to free Jeremy Bamber and James (Shay) Power. In fact Shay Power was released from prison, his conviction for armed robbery overturned by the Court of Appeal, on December 21, 2004, exactly 23 years after the murder for which Reyos was convicted.

As a result of all of this I had not had the opportunity to properly look at Reyos' case when, in January 2005, he emailed me again to ask, 'Scott, I am inquiring if you are interested in the James Harry Reyos case in Texas. If so, please let me know.'

My other campaigns, and my attempts of have more of my work published, had meant that I did not properly begin to examine the facts of Reyos' case until April 2005 and only then in between trying to secure a deal with a publisher for a book about Jeremy Bamber, and in between helping with a General Election campaign.

It was in early April that Reyos, in what I was soon to learn was his characteristic persistence, contacted me again to urge me to look into his case:

'Dear Scott: I emailed you once before concerning my wrongful conviction in the United States, in State of Texas. I believe that I am reaching a point where JUSTICE will finally prevail after nearly 23 years. I hope that Governor Rick Perry will sign my Pardon Petition, which is currently sitting on his desk. He must, in order for JUSTICE to prevail. I will keep you posted. Thank you for your time. James Harry Reyos.'

This time I listened and answered his call. I was, however, confused about how a convicted killer could be contacting me, although I am aware some prisoners do have limited access to the internet but thought it more likely that he, like many other prisoners, had a supporter on the outside who was typing out his letters and sending them by email in order to save him postage costs.

However, I soon learnt that Reyos was no longer in prison, having been released on parole. It was a strange concept because in Britain those who protest their innocence for murder (In Denial of Murder is the term used by the authorities) are very rarely released on parole, although it is becoming a little more common here. He told me:

'I am now living in Austin, at an apartment complex. I enjoy my limited freedom, however, I am looking forward to being exonerated and pardoned so that I can have full liberty to go anywhere I want instead of being limited in my movements.'

I had only a basic knowledge of how the American justice system worked (in fact I still do not really understand it because it is very different to the British system) and so was unsure how I could help, other than helping to spread the facts. Reyos' case was very different to the campaigns to overturn convictions for murders, armed robberies and other serious offences I have worked on in Britain because I understand how the legal system here works, and how mistakes can (in theory) be remedied through the appeals process. I had to admit to Reyos that I did not think I could do very much for him.

Nonetheless Reyos was very persistent and persuasive and if there was any truth in his claims then I could not see how he could be responsible. I had to know more and take whatever action I could.

In response to my doubts about how I could be helpful, Reyos had a suggestion for me, 'Perhaps, Scott, you can help spread the word via the internet.' He also asked how he could get hold of a copy of my book on the Barry George case, a copy of which I later gave him, and spoke about how he would like to write his own story. 'I am hoping to write my own book too, once I get this pardon.', he told me. His email ended:

> 'I believe that I have a very compelling story to tell of the criminal justice system here in the United States. I greatly appreciate your time and assistance. Sincerely, James Harry Reyos.'

I began to research the case in detail and was surprised how much information was available online, in the form of digitized newspapers from the 1980s (although sadly Google has since removed many of these free to view newspapers) as well as more recent news stories from the 1990s and early 2000s relating to his campaign. Reyos was also able to provide photocopies of reports and trial transcripts, and to succinctly outline the key aspects of the cases for and against him. It was clear to me that Reyos is a seasoned campaigner who can convincingly argue the flaws in his conviction, to anyone who would listen. He had to hope that the authorities in Texas, and specifically the State Governor and the Texas Board of Pardons and Paroles would listen. He was determined to make his voice heard.

'I believe that I am reaching a point where justice will finally prevail, after nearly twenty three years.', Reyos told me in April 2005, adding:

> 'I have composed a three-page letter to the Texas Board of Pardons and Paroles. I am hoping that they review the letter with an open mind and make a positive decision to the Governor of Texas concerning the Pardon Petition that is currently on his desk. I hope that Governor Rick Perry will sign my Pardon Petition. He must, in order for justice to prevail.

While I am being punished for this brutal crime, the real killer is still free. When is this injustice going to end? I continue to fight this injustice because I know in my heart I am truly innocent. I did not kill Father Patrick Ryan!'

His letter to the Board of Pardons and Paroles explained the key aspect of his defense: the alibi. It also referred to Dennis Cadra's support, despite Cadra having been the prosecuting attorney at Reyos' appeal. 'JUSTICE must prevail soon.', he wrote to me.

Reyos' letter to the Board of Pardons and Paroles was written following discussions with a State Representative, Paul Moreno, at the State Capitol. He felt confident that his efforts and those of his supporters, myself included now that I was beginning to write about the case, would result in the Board looking again at the validity of the jury's verdict. 'I believe that people need to be apprised of this gross miscarriage of justice in Texas.', he wrote on April 11.

One week later Reyos was in very high spirits, having met with Representative Moreno. Reyos had been excited, though outwardly fairly calm and collected as is his style, as he listened to Moreno explain what was happening with regards to his petition. Moreno was able to say that there was a 98% chance that the Governor, Rick Perry, would rule in Reyos' favor and ask the Board of Pardons and Paroles to review the case and grant a full pardon on the grounds of innocence. 'Within the next month and a half, I believe something good will happen.', he wrote, adding, 'Maybe the heat and pressure from supporters will be put on the top leadership of Texas and result in my exoneration and pardon.' Reyos gave me Moreno's email address and so I contacted him.

Reyos told me again at this time that he was keen to write a book once he was pardoned, to expose the injustices in the USA and because he has 'a very good story, very interesting and intriguing'.

A few days later he visited the State Capitol again and spoke with Mike Lopez, hoping to hear some encouraging news regarding a decision from the Board of Pardons and Paroles. He was informed that the Board would make contact within two or three weeks. 'We believe that the Board will have no alternative but to make a favorable ruling to Texas Governor Rick Perry with a Full Pardon Based Upon Innocence.', he told me. Reyos was given a copy of the letter which State Representative Moreno had sent the Board and Reyos was excited to read it, believing it to be 'powerful'.

Indeed it was a powerful letter from Moreno, requesting that the Board of Pardons and Paroles hold a formal hearing to review Reyos' case. Reyos sent me a copy of the letter. In the letter Moreno expressed his dismay at the Board's previous decision (in 1992) had been made following only an informal meeting which could not possibly have acquainted itself with the necessary information and facts to make an appropriate recommendation to the Governor. In fact the members of the Board had voted by fax; they had not even been in the same building to discuss the case and they were not fully acquainted with the facts. 'As a matter of public confidence in the process, the Board can address the considerable amount of reasonable doubt that lingers in this case.', he wrote.

I began sending letters to the media in the USA as well as in Britain and Ireland, to raise awareness and to hope that favorable publicity could lead to the Board feeling the need to do what was right.

In Britain and Ireland the story made the national press, with articles in the *Irish Mirror* newspaper and also the *Irish Evening Herald* and the *Limerick Leader*. I knew that my efforts would not help directly with influencing any decisions regarding Reyos' case, but I hoped that some additional publicity for the wrongful conviction would be good. I also hoped to find information about Father Ryan and believed this could originate from his native Ireland. Father Ryan was such a mysterious character and I felt sure there was someone who must know more about his background, which could have some bearing on why he was killed and which could corroborate the evidence that Father Ryan was a man who preyed on young men.

Reyos naturally was also promoting his case, contacting hundreds of journalists and attempting to have his campaign's profile raised in print, online, on radio and on television. His efforts were hugely successful and for a time there must have been thousands of people talking about his case as a direct result. He spoke with a number of investigative journalists, which resulted in his story being broadcast on KEYE TV 42, KTSM TV and interest from other media. He was particularly pleased with the KEYE TV 42 news piece, which he felt was 'a powerful story about my wrongful conviction.' This program also featured Paul Moreno.

'I believe that the media is gearing up for the final decision (which I hope is favorable) that the Board of Pardons and Paroles will make to Governor Rick Perry.', he told me.

In between the media interviews Reyos continued to lobby politicians and tried to remain calm despite what appeared to be growing momentum for his exoneration. 'I am doing fine, still taking one day at a time.', he told me on May 2, adding:

> 'I am waiting patiently for the final decision from the Board of Pardons and Paroles. ... Believe me, Scott, I am very excited that my case is now before the Board being reviewed. However, I am keeping my hopes at an even level, because a few times before my high hopes have been dashed and that feeling of disappointment is very hurtful.'

After 22 years of fighting to clear his name it was no wonder that Reyos had suffered many occasions of being seriously hurt when his innocence has been ignored despite overwhelming evidence of an injustice. This time we had to do everything we could in order to make sure the hurt was not felt again.

On May 6, Reyos again visited the State Capitol to attend a meeting with Moreno in order to see if there had been any developments. The meeting was cancelled due to the tragic news of a motor accident which, earlier that day, had claimed the life of one of the State Representatives. Reyos did, however, manage to briefly speak with Moreno's aide and as a result he learned that a response was yet to arrive from the Board of Pardons and Paroles and until a response was received there was little that Moreno or his office could do. The office was keen not to pressurize the Board for fear of receiving the wrong response.

Reyos was pleased with the publicity in his case and even more so when the Survivors Network of those Abused by Priests agreed to support him by writing to the Board of Pardons and Paroles. 'I am hoping that the great amount of attention will ultimately force the top leadership of the State of Texas to exonerate me and pardon me.', Reyos told me.

By May 23 the waiting was becoming too much for Reyos. They must find in his favor, he wrote, because of the 'overwhelming evidence in my file indicating innocence.' He would consider legal action against the Board if it did not find in his favor. 'Let's hope that the increased publicity will pressure the top leadership of Texas to act appropriately, promptly and, of course, justly. The ONLY just decision that the Board can recommend is Full Pardon Based Upon Innocence.'

It was the support he was receiving from his supporters, and the interest from the media, in particular the *Austin Chronicle* which he was excited to tell me would publish his story in the first or second week of June, that was keeping him going, although as always he told me that he was 'fine and well' before adding, 'We are still waiting on a response from the Board of Pardons and Paroles. We hope it will be made soon.'

Two days later I received another email. It was May 25, Reyos' birthday, and he was certainly trying to make the best he could of his birthday, although his disappointment at more waiting, and his feelings of injustice were preventing any form of celebration. He asked me to contact the Board of Pardons and Paroles again, which I did that same day. I was determined to give Reyos at least some hope on his birthday.

He was particularly annoyed that he would not be able to leave his apartment on Memorial Day, which was to be held on Monday May 30, it being a public holiday. 'No movement will be allowed for any parolee on that day.', he wrote, adding:

> 'That's what is very unjust: me, a truly innocent man being treated this way, not being able to be totally free. That's certainly not right – while the real killer roams free, committing more crime. Scott, I am truly indebted to you for your sincere interest in my case, and for taking the time to assist me in my fight for justice. I only wish that there were more people like you who advocate "justice." It doesn't take a "rocket scientist" to detect an error in a wrongful conviction, but it's the system (those people in power) who don't like to admit a mistake was made, because of the subsequent consequences. They would rather allow an injustice to linger than to take the necessary steps to rectify it. That's a shame. I just can't see how anyone in

a position like that (who allows an injustice to linger) can sleep at night. One day they will have to face the Great Spirit to answer for their actions, or lack of. I can only pray that the Great Spirit will have mercy upon them. I am a person who can forgive those who have wronged me. I believe that is a mandate that the Great Spirit gives all of us. It's left up to us, as individuals, to forgive or not. Plus, I think that forgiving a person allows you, as a person, to begin the healing process for the hurt done and allow you to move forward in a positive way, instead of having a negative and vengeful attitude. That's what's wrong with our society today; nobody is willing to forgive others. Well, Scott, I just thought I'd give you a little of my thoughts and feelings. I look forward to hearing from you. …'

I contacted lots more media and politicians, as did Reyos and his other supporters. In an email to me on June 1, he wrote that he felt sure the publicity drive would help his case:

'Hopefully it will reach someone who will take notice of the injustice that I am going through. In a few days (on June 10th) will mark the 22nd anniversary of my conviction.',

He told me had already written some letters and was planning on writing letters to editors of newspapers, so that those letters could be printed in the newspapers.

One of his letters had received a positive response, which greatly encouraged him in his fight. The letter had been sent to an Amarillo based attorney named Jeff Blackburn and as a result he received a phone call from Blackburn. Reyos was excited to have Blackburn's interest because he was one of the attorneys who helped the Tulia citizens get pardoned after being wrongfully convicted of trafficking drugs. Blackburn had started an innocence project at Texas Tech University in Lubbock, Texas and, according to Reyos, he was 'extremely interested in helping me with my case.'

As I understand the *Austin Chronicle* were also instrumental in obtaining Blackburn's interest in the case. Reyos asked me to contact Blackburn, which I did, and he and I exchanged several emails about Reyos' case.

A few days before sending me this email, Reyos had again visited the State Capitol for an update on the petition to the Board of Pardons and Paroles. Moreno informed him that no news had been received, and they were still waiting for a response. However, there was some positive news in that the 79th Legislature was now over and so Moreno could devote more time to Reyos' case. He was considering putting some pressure on the Board for a response.

Although the waiting was causing disappointment and frustration there were many positives for Reyos at this time in addition to Jeff Blackburn's interest in the case. Whilst at the State Capitol a reporter from the *Austin Chronicle* named Jordan Smith met with Reyos and took some photographs to accompany the major feature she was writing for that publication, and interviewed him at great length. She also arranged to visit Reyos in his apartment in order to take more photographs and to gain a better understanding of him. Reyos was instantly impressed by her and felt sure that the feature she was writing would be instrumental in his campaign. Jordan remains a strong supporter of Reyos' to this day. He was extremely excited about the article and could not wait to read it.

Reyos was becoming somewhat of a local celebrity and was certainly enjoying the attention, but only in the hope that it would lead to his wrongful conviction being highlighted further so that the authorities would be shamed into rectifying it. 'I have been getting comments from strangers off the streets about the KEYE 42 NEWS story.', he told me, adding:

> 'Many can't believe that I was convicted of a crime I did not commit, and spent 21 years in prison for it. They believe that the justice system is very unfair and badly needs repair. I concur!'

On June 2, Reyos called Moreno's office and was delighted to hear that there were "rumors" that Governor Perry was intending to sign the Pardon Petition. If true this was fantastic news and would have led to Reyos' conviction being overturned. Having been disappointed many times in the past, however, Reyos did not want to believe that the rumors were true. He told me:

'My case is being used as a political football, tossed around with no definite result. ... I am keeping calm, despite the uncertainty of what might happen. I wish that they will just go ahead and pardon me and get this over. Everyday that goes by, is just one more day that JUSTICE is denied to a truly innocent man.'

There were two other developments which gave him grounds for optimism. Firstly, the *Austin Chronicle* article, which was scheduled to be published on June 10 and, secondly, Blackburn informed Reyos that he would meet him in 'several weeks' to discuss the case and see what he could do to help. I had written another letter to the Board of Pardons and Paroles and Reyos was grateful for this. 'I hope that they heed the facts proving innocence that you pointed out. Sooner or later, they will have to respond to Rep. Moreno's letter. It can't go unanswered forever.', he told me, adding, 'I know you can plainly see the gross miscarriage of justice exhibited in my case: why can't the top leadership of Texas see it too?'

The *Austin Chronicle* article was delayed by a week, but it was worth the extra wait. Reyos was very happy when he read it and emailed me on the morning to tell me about the 'compelling story' which Jordan Smith had written. He felt confident it would help his cause:

'I am hoping that it will now capture the attention of those in power, and the public, to show the gross miscarriage of justice plainly exhibited in my case. I will keep you posted on any feedback I get from the story. I also saw the story on another emailing post. So maybe the exposure will put pressure on the top leadership of Texas to act, to pardon me.'

In the *Austin Chronicle* article Jeff Blackburn duly was quoted as saying:

"I think we can do a total turnaround here. This case is constitutionally reprehensible. When there's this much injustice there must be a way to get it overturned. It may be torturous, but we'll do it."

A few days after it was printed Reyos sent me a copy of the *Austin Chronicle*, containing the feature of his case, along with a letter and other information about his case, including some older magazine articles that had highlighted his fight to clear his name. The *Austin Chronicle* feature was certainly very substantial and impressive, spread over eight pages under the title of 'Who Killed Father Ryan?' It also formed the cover story of the publication, with a large photograph of Reyos. The article detailed the facts of the case and Reyos' parole conditions emphasizing the fact that although he was at that time free on parole he still did not have true freedom. I had read the article online but Reyos wanted to make sure I had a copy of the actual publication.

Reyos obtained a large amount of new support off the back of the *Austin Chronicle* article and he hoped the momentum would continue but he was not getting carried away. He knew there had always been reasonable doubt in his case and that the article provided information which the jury at his trial had heard, and had chosen to ignore. He told me on June 20:

> 'I believe that the information will certainly put the thought of "reasonable doubt" in my guilt in the crime. Of course, during the trial there was always reasonable doubt. However, the jury chose to ignore the powerful evidence proving innocence. They definitely reached the wrong verdict.',

There was more to the article than a précis of Reyos' case. It gave some information about the type of man Reyos is and, importantly, it mentioned a man who has become known as the Boise Doe. This man, who is detailed in a later chapter, committed suicide almost a year after Father Ryan's murder and it has been speculated that he could have been involved in the murder of Father Ryan as well as similar murders of other Catholic priests, which are detailed in later chapters.

Reyos feels sure the Boise Doe was involved in Father Ryan's murder and feels that if the jury had heard about him, they may have had more doubt about the prosecution's case:

> 'I wish that the Boise John Doe information was available during the trial; we could've used it to further prove my

innocence. Then again, who knows if the jury would've bothered to take that information into consideration.'

Reyos had been asked a series of questions by students from the Innocence Project, who were working with Jeff Blackburn. He told me:

'I am glad that I have their support, and that they are willing to take on my case. I believe with Jeff's assistance I will get some action, along with Rep. Moreno's support and assistance.'

He was also pleased that a special session had been called to discuss a school finance bill. This would mean that all of the State Representatives would be in Austin and he was hoping to use this as an opportunity to lobby them in order to gain further support for his campaign. He felt confident, sharing his thoughts with me:

'I still wait patiently for justice to prevail. I know it is on the horizon. ... I will continue to take one day at a time. It's difficult at times not knowing "when" something is going to happen. This past Saturday the Texas controller announced that she is running for governor, so maybe that will be good – a change of leadership here in Texas. ...'

Reyos appealed to the Governor, Rick Perry, but given that his letters to Perry had gone unanswered he decided to send the letter to the *Austin Chronicle*, and it was printed on the letter page. He hoped that this way the Governor would see it and have to respond. Reyos' letter was printed on June 24, 2005 and read:

'Turning a blind eye to justice affects everyone. As Martin Luther King said, "Injustice anywhere is a threat to justice everywhere." I was wrongly convicted, more than 22 years ago, for the murder of Father Patrick Ryan in Odessa. Why can't a truly innocent man get justice? Is there a double standard of justice here in Texas?
When something goes wrong in the criminal justice system, it's never too late to try to correct the mistake. Sooner or later justice must prevail. In my wrongful conviction case the

ultimate outcome – which should be full pardon based upon innocence – is now left up to the top leadership of Texas, namely the Board of Pardons and Paroles and the governor. Are they going to continue to deny justice to an innocent man? Or are they going to take the necessary steps to correct this obvious wrongful conviction?

I would like to think – and believe wholeheartedly! – that Gov. Perry would strongly adhere to his statement that he made (as quoted in the Fort Worth Star-Telegram, Jan 18, 2001) regarding correcting wrongful convictions: "Either we will confirm the previous findings of a jury, or we will correct a grave injustice in instances where the wrong person has been convicted."

I humbly appeal to you, Gov. Perry, to intervene and help bring my wrongful conviction to an end.

Don't give me the deaf ear, governor!

Don't ignore my cry of innocence, governor!

Don't ignore my call for justice, governor!

Don't allow my wrongful conviction to linger on and on and on, governor!

One thing is for certain, and has been proven to be true: I did not kill Father Patrick Ryan. I was innocent yesterday! I am innocent today! And, I will be innocent in perpetuity!'

Characteristically Governor Rick Perry gave Reyos the deaf ear once again and ignored the letter. There was growing interest in the media, however, with Reyos frequently being interviewed. The media in Boise, Idaho, had taken an interest because of the reference to the Boise Doe in the *Austin Chronicle*. The interest from Boise had left Reyos 'quite excited'. He was also pleased with the Innocence Project and interest he was receiving from the students. 'Jeff's Innocence Project at Texas Tech is very interested in my case and I believe they will pursue it to the end. I will keep you posted on any further developments.', he wrote on June 27, adding that he was still waiting to hear from the Board of Pardons and Paroles and 'I hope that justice prevails soon.'

On June 29, Reyos was out looking for a job. With all of the developments in his case his job hunting had been pushed back a little but he was determined to find work. He had received my book,

The Case of Barry George, that day and was looking forward to reading it. Reyos has always taken a great interest in those who are also fighting to clear their name.

He was still excited that Blackburn was involved in his campaign. He was also optimistic having spoken with Mike Lopez about developments. Lopez had informed Reyos that another State Representative, Terri Hodge, had joined his fight for justice. 'She is located here in Austin and has written several letters to the Board of Pardons and Paroles. She is a very outspoken person when it comes to criminal justice issues.' Lopez had also told him that things were moving slowly towards justice.

There were encouraging signs but the waiting was proving difficult. Reyos had spent 23 years campaigning to clear his name, and had had to endure lengthy waits on many occasions, but waiting for a response from the Board of Pardons and Paroles this time was agonizing. 'I continue to take one day at a time.', he told me on July 1, adding:

> 'Yes, the waiting for justice to prevail is nerve-racking, not knowing what's going to happen and when it's going to happen. I have a lot of patience, however. I will keep calm through the storm. I am very grateful that I have the Great Spirit on my side too. He is in complete control of all events.'

He was taking an interest in the Barry George case, having begun reading my book, and told me about his hopes and plans in helping others once he had secured his pardon:

> 'I hope to one day help those who have been wrongly convicted, but for now I really can't do too much with my limited movements, contacts etc. I have always thought about starting my own organization to help those innocent people, even helping inmates who have been released from prison. It's hard to get back on your feet (like I am currently experiencing) with a number on your back (especially when you have a serious offense). One thing is for certain, though, you cannot give up. I want to be a person who encourages others to continue to fight for your freedom. It's quite encouraging to me that Barry is continuing his fight for justice. The way I believe

if you are truly innocent you don't give up your fight. That's something you know in your heart to be true; your innocence. People may have their doubts about your innocence but if you are truly innocent you fight until you clear your name. If I had never fought my case I wouldn't be where I am now with the support I have from many people (including you, Scott). I truly believe that JUSTICE is on the horizon. I will remain patient for justice to prevail.'

He was disappointed that American Independence Day, that day where the USA celebrates its freedom, was approaching, but that he would have to spend three days locked in his apartment because of the rules preventing him from going outdoors on a public holiday.

In July 2005 I worked away from my home, in a city in the north of England called York, famous for its connections to the Vikings. I was only away for two weeks, carrying out an archaeological excavation, and so I had two weeks away from campaigning for Reyos and the many others whose fights for justice were supported by me. It was whilst I was away, on July 7, that terrorists carried out attacks on a bus and the underground tube system in London, killing more than 50 people, injuring many more and causing uncountable fear amongst the people of London and the whole of my country.

I had no internet access during this time but when I returned home I found some concerned emails from Reyos, one of which read:

'Stay safe. The incidents in London I've been watching on cable TV. It's horrible that such things happen in our world. I wish that we can all just get along with each other, expressing our love and care for one another, instead of hate and violence. It saddens me that our world is like it is, filled with violence. Please stay safe.'

In York I was more than 200 miles away from the devastation and the only evidence I saw of anything amiss was two police officers gossiping at York Railway Station. They had been placed there to form a police presence and be on guard should any other terrorist activity take place at that train station, yet Osama Bin Laden himself could have walked straight past and the police officers would have been oblivious, such was their level of vigilance.

That day, on the other side of the world, my country and I were in the thoughts of Reyos. It was very typical of Reyos, considering others even as he faced his own difficulties. He sent me another email the next day:

> 'Dear Scott, yesterday I mailed you a card and several large envelopes with information about my case. I hope you receive them soon and please let me know when you get them, I am very sorry about your country's terrible incident. It's sad that we have people in this world who will harm people. I hope your country stands strong against these crazy people. My heartfelt wishes go out to everybody in Great Britain. Please stay safe. I know the Great Spirit is watching over you. I will check my email Monday 7/11. I hope you are having a nice vacation. Take care Scott. Sincerely, James.'

As with the emails I received the packages when I returned from the excavation. The first bulky package of information was dated July 4, 2005, when Reyos was locked in his apartment unable to celebrate freedom. He was using this temporary imprisonment as an opportunity to work on his case and compile information. It was the first mailing I had had from him through 'snail mail.' His letters whilst out of prison were almost always typed, well presented and had immaculate spelling, punctuation and grammar. They often had colorful lines as borders. It was immediately clear that Reyos was a man for whom presentation was extremely important.

His first letter opened:

> 'Dear Scott, Greetings! I truly hope that this missive finds you fine and well. By the time you get this letter, you will have been back from your vacation. I hope that you had a wonderful and fun time.'

It was work rather than a vacation, but it mattered not. In this letter he referred to having sent two other packages of documents but I only received one of them. He also referred to sending a thank you card and some photographs, which I thankfully did receive. The card had been ripped in half which I found to be strange. Indeed it was apparent that the envelope had been opened and so clearly the package had been intercepted and tampered with which I found to be a matter of high concern. Perhaps it was opened by customs officers but why would they rip a card? There were several photographs including a recent one of Reyos stood in front of the State Capitol. He had a big smile on his face. I imagine he had the photograph specifically taken to send to me. Reyos had written on the photograph, saying 'To Scott, Best wishes!' and had signed his name. The other photographs included a Native American quilt, the Texas State Capitol, Congress Avenue Bridge in Austin and scenes of El Paso, where he had lived before moving to Austin: a Native American sculpture in front of the Speaking Rock Casino on the Pueblo del Suv Indian Reservation; El Paso County Law Library where Reyos used to carry out legal research for his case; a photograph of El Paso showing the Franklyn Mountains. This latter photograph was taken by Reyos as he stood in the El Paso law library, which was on the 12th floor of the County Library.

In his letter he informed me that having read my book on the Barry George case he wanted to support Barry and would include him in his prayers. It was so typical of Reyos' caring and loving nature.

His letter ended in typical fashion:

'I wish you well, and success, in all your endeavors, Scott. I pray that the Great Spirit will richly bless you. Also, thank you for all that you have done for me. You are a young man with much sincerity and integrity. My best wishes to you. Sincerely, James Harry Reyos.'

Reyos may have been grateful for what I had done to that point, but I was determined to do much more for him, and his packages of information were to form a good starting point.

Reyos was still trying to find work in between his campaigning activities and was longing to be pardoned so that he would return to the beautiful mountains of New Mexico to see those green fields and mountains and to experience the warm summers and bitter cold and snowy winters that he loves so much. He wanted some photos of Britain, and of me, and I sent him a few. Reyos has always been interested in different cultures and was interested to see what life was like in Britain.

On July 25, Reyos returned to the State Capitol where he learnt that the Board of Pardons and Paroles had finally responded to Moreno's letter. Moreno had written three months earlier and had taken a second letter to enquire why a response had not been sent, before anything was heard. No decision had been made but they at least had acknowledged receipt of the letters and said that they were considering the case.

Whilst at the State Capitol Reyos used the opportunity to speak with other State Representatives, having sent letters to them all, in order to see whether he could count on their support. Representative Harold Dutton, who Reyos described as 'a man of great integrity, siding on the side of justice for those who have been wronged', expressed his interest in the case and told Reyos that he would lend his time and assistance. He spoke very briefly with Representative Keel, who showed some interest. He also met Representative Terri Hodge, who was surprised to meet him in person, but reaffirmed her support. Dutton and Hodge spent around an hour and a half with Reyos and during their meeting they spoke to Jeff Blackburn. The phone was on loud speaker so that everyone could converse together during the 20 minute call. Reyos was very excited to hear Blackburn say that he was moving forward with his research and was preparing his argument for the Board. He believed it would be another two or three months before the case was presented to the Board and there were some political "heavyweights" who were joining the call for Reyos to be exonerated.

'So, I think that the Board will have no choice but to recommend to Governor Perry the ultimate decision: Full Pardon Based Upon Innocence.', Reyos told me after the meeting, adding:

> 'So, Scott, things are slowly moving ahead. Right now, Attorney Blackburn doesn't want too much attention on the case but will when the time approaches to present the case to the Board. Like I've been told, they will have no chance but to consider the substantial and credible evidence proving my case. I will keep you posted on developments. Take care, Scott. I believe things are going to end in a favorable manner. The

support is building. My best wishes to you. May the Great Spirit bless you and keep you safe.'

A few days later Reyos spoke to Mike Lopez who told him that he, Lopez, was feeling confident that things would go favorably to Reyos and that support was growing. 'So I am feeling more confident too. However, I am still keeping an even level on my hopes. I think, though, things are moving forward in a good way.', Reyos told me after the phone call.

At this time I felt Reyos needed his own website so that he had a greater voice, with the ability to post his own messages online for the world to see. I had an input, and later ran, the Barry George website and also helped with other websites for prisoners in Britain. I had actually set up quite a few and as my knowledge of building websites increased I became more confident in setting them up. Reyos was initially concerned and whilst not entirely against the idea he needed some persuasion. The reason for this was that he had read an article in The Statesman about prisoners who had their own websites and had heard that there was a lot of public anger towards prisoners being given a voice. Nonetheless he himself used the media, including television appearances, and I felt sure that if he saw a website and agreed with its content he would recognize the potential benefits for his plight.

On August 1, I built a website and sent Reyos a link. His initial concerns were instantly overcome when he saw the site and he was overjoyed to have his own space online where people could learn the facts 'I believe that my own website will help publicize my case and, hopefully, gain more supporters now that my case is fixin' to be presented to the Board.'

He was receiving positive vibes when speaking with Moreno's office, telling me:

> 'Yes, I am a little excited knowing that my case will soon be presented to the Board, and the rather good news from Rep Moreno's office (and others) that the chances of exoneration and subsequent pardon are looking favorable. Of course, too, I am keeping calm because I don't want to get overly optimistic and then have my high hopes dashed because of a denial. I am keeping an even-level attitude; "cool, calm and collected."

He added that he was hoping to hear from Blackburn soon, 'I know he is extremely busy putting the arguments together to present to the Board.'

In a rare display of anger Reyos told me he had to cut his email short because he had to visit his Parole Officer in order to arrange his weekly schedule of movements and activities. This particularly annoyed him:

> 'That's something that I cannot get over. Here I am – a truly innocent man being monitored – while the real killer still roams free, completely free! Possibly committing more crimes. Nevertheless I continue to keep a positive attitude. I try to keep focused on my goals in life. I know, one day soon, I will be a free man. I have never lost hope, and faith, that that day will come.'

On August 5 he received encouraging news from Blackburn's office. Blackburn had been in contact with Father Ryan's brother who had disclosed some interesting information relevant to the case. Unfortunately Reyos did not know the information but he was greatly encouraged by this development. Reyos was told that everyone was "pretty optimistic" about the information and that Blackburn was putting together a 'strong argument and presentation' which should be ready by the end of October. Reyos told me:

> 'I will continue to wait patiently for it to be presented. Jeff is thinking of having me present at the hearing so that the Board will see me in person (to put a human face to the case). ... I think things are slowly moving in the right direction. It's slow, but in the right direction. I am glad. I will continue to keep calm and patient.'

Whilst he endured the ongoing wait there was welcome relief in that his job hunting was progressing well. He had applied for a number of jobs and had been offered an interview on August 8, telling me, 'I am rather excited about that, that I will, hopefully, get a job.' Very soon after he had a second interview. Regarding the first, he later told me:

'I went to my job interview and it went quite well. They will be contacting me soon if I am offered the job. Things looked, and sounded, quite promising during the interview; however, I will just have to wait and see if they seriously considered me. That was only one interview that I had. I am still waiting on an answer from another one.'

He was also greatly encouraged by numerous very recent cases which had been shown to be wrongful convictions, sharing with me the stories of some of these. Thomas Doswell had spent 19 years in prison in Pittsburgh for rape but DNA evidence proved his innocence. Luis Diaz spent 26 years in prison in Miami for a series of rapes but was exonerated. He was watching a program on FOX about the case of Marty Tankleff who was believed to have been wrongfully convicted of murdering his parents. This pleased Reyos, who wrote to me saying:

'So, maybe, with all the publicity of these cases of wrongful convictions my case will be given some attention. Who knows, my case might be the next high-profile case to get overturned. I continue to wait patiently. Yes, it is difficult at times, but I have the Great Spirit on my side giving me patience, understanding, and His love and care.'

During August I traveled down to Suffolk, in the south of England, where I worked on an archaeological excavation for two months. During this time I stayed in a cottage on farmland, several miles from the nearest town and the only internet access was when I was able to visit the local library, very briefly, after work. The library was rarely open, however. I did, though, go home twice for weekends and was able to catch up with Reyos on these occasions.

During one of my infrequent internet sessions I was delighted to hear some positive news from Reyos. 'I now have a job, which I enjoy very much.', he told me, having been appointed a Houseman at Mansion At Judges Hill, a 5 star hotel and restaurant. It was a 45 minute bus journey to work but this did not bother him very much. With his new job there was an increase in confidence and optimism.

He later sent me a pamphlet advertising the premises, and it was clear he had great pride in his new job.

He loved his work and he proved to be a popular member of staff. Jack Bartlett, the Director of Operations at The Mansion, would later write:

> 'I am very lucky to have hired James. He is always on time and ready to work. He is a wonderful person to work with and get to know. I am very often amazed by the things he has been through, and how he always has a smile and a great attitude towards everything he does.'

The supervising houseman, Andrew Burrell, agreed, writing:

> 'I have had the opportunity to work with James Reyos. He has shown himself to be an efficient, reliable and conscientious employee. I consider James to be an asset to the staff.'

Indeed Reyos was awarded employee of the month soon after starting work and was offered the position of supervisor, which he turned down because he believed his name would soon be cleared and that he could then return to New Mexico.

I returned home, from Suffolk, during early October and soon received an email, on October 9, in which Reyos told me:

> 'Things are slowly moving forward. I have been in contact with my attorney Jeff Blackburn, and he is preparing for the presentation and argument before the Board in late November or early December. I am getting a little excited, but I am keeping calm though.'

He sent me a list of email addresses of media, politicians and organizations dealing with injustices, and asked me to contact them all in order to publicize the website and to let people know of developments in the case. He added:

> 'I believe that Mr Blackburn is going to "drop a bombshell" on the Board with the information that he is getting from his

investigation, which is very positive. Whenever that happens, it will be big news. I am keeping calm through it all.'

Reyos had been very busy with work, working long hours, and with his restrictions on his movements his access to the internet was becoming increasingly limited. We exchanged letters via the mail but we did not contact each other as much as we had done. My own work, working away from home, had made the problem much worse. However, I was soon to start working only 40 miles from home and was able to commute each day. At this time he wrote to me:

'I am just getting off work now and decided to come to the dayroom to check my emails. This doesn't happen very often, as you can see. I really miss spending more time with you via emails. I know you understand the situation though. Please write to me via snail mail. I'll get it sooner. No telling when I can get on the computer again.'

As October progressed there was another delay but this did not concern Reyos. It transpired that an associate of Jeff Blackburn was going to fly out to California in order to speak to Father Ryan's brother. The brother had been in contact with Blackburn and some relevant information had come to light, but this needed to be verified and more detail was required. Upon learning of the delay, Reyos told me it could work in his favor:

'I think it is good that the pardon petition will be presented in late November or early December – the closer it is to the anniversary of the crime the better (the more publicity).'.

However, as October became November there was still no news. There was still no news as such on November 3 when Reyos wrote to me again:

'I have never heard from Mr Blackburn lately, but I am sure he is quite busy finishing up his research for the Pardon Petition. Last phone call that I received from him, he said that things were going quite well, that things were looking "very positive"., He had no idea when the presentation to the Board would take place, but he was told that a special prosecutor would be appointed, who would be granted unlimited powers to investigate all aspects of the case.'

Reyos was pleased that political support was growing and that a number of State Representatives from his home state of New Mexico had been in touch with Blackburn in order to offer their support. Reyos began circulating a campaign leaflet I produced for him, sending it to politicians in Texas and New Mexico.

A few days later, on November 7, he had still not heard any news. 'I am getting ready for Mr Blackburn's presentation, even though I still do not know the exact date. … I am hoping for the best of course.', he told me.

As the days passed it became apparent a presentation would not be taking place in November. On November 10 he wrote me a brief email, because he had had a hectic day at work although he told me he enjoyed being busy. Due to being so busy he did not have time to write in proper English. Part of the email read:

> 'I will B writing 2 Mr Blackburn tomorrow to request a date 4 his presentation. I will contact U when I get that firm date. I truly believe that justice will prevail. … Things R looking up. Again, thank U 4 all that U have done. U R 2 B commended 4 your unselfish acts. Believe me, there needs 2 B more people like U in this unsettling world. Well, I will end 4 now. Take care. May the Great Spirit richly bless U! sincerely, James.'

After November 10 I did not hear from Reyos for a few weeks, which was unusual so I became worried. I sent him a number of emails and letters but received no response until a little over a month later. I was relieved to learn there was nothing wrong, but that he had been busy at work.

It was on December 15 that he wrote:

> 'Dear Scott, please don't fret, everything is fine with me. Glad that you are concern for me. I am still waiting for justice to prevail. I believe it will prevail soon. Mr Blackburn called me and gave me some encouraging news. Things are looking very positive.'

He went on to tell me that there had been more media interest but that Blackburn had not wanted to ruffle any feathers and so Reyos was not allowed to give any interviews. He was anxious to follow Blackburn's advice. His letter continued:

> 'Believe me Scott it will happen soon. Mr Blackburn told me that the only media interview that I will conduct is "on the front steps of the Ector County Courthouse when you are exonerated and pardoned." I am getting a little nervous, but I am still maintaining my composure.'

He was, as I say, working very hard at work but it was paying off. He received a raise and a certificate recognizing his excellent job performance.

As the year came to an end there was no news on when Reyos' case was to be presented to the Texas Board of Pardons and Paroles but news from Blackburn gave him encouragement and his work at the Mansion House helped keep his spirits. With the New Year there would be renewed hope that Reyos would receive the recognition through the justice system that he was an innocent man.

The view from the 12th floor of the El Paso County Law Library, where Reyos spent time working on his case. The Franklin Mountains are in the background. (Photograph taken by James Harry Reyos)

The Texas State Capitol, where Reyos spent many hours speaking with State Representatives (photograph taken by James Harry Reyos)

New Hope

The year 2006 started in what Reyos described as a 'very positive' way. Jeff Blackburn had met with the Ector County District Attorney, John W. Smith, who had represented Reyos at his trial in 1983. The meeting had been positive, with a special prosecutor being appointed. On January 31 Reyos wrote:

> 'The S.P. [special prosecutor] is now in the process of conducting his investigation into the case. Also, Mr Blackburn will be filing a writ of habeas corpus on February 22, 2006. A federal district judge will be assigned to hear the case. Things are looking "very positive" so far. I am very excited about the latest developments.'

He went on to say:

> 'I truly hope that the justice system recognizes the gross miscarriage of justice plainly exhibited in my case. If there is such a thing as "justice" here in Texas, then once the media attention begins I believe the public will see the gross miscarriage of justice in my case.'

He added that he was very busy at work but that he still greatly enjoyed his job. His letter ended with his renewed hope and belief that his conviction would be overturned, 'I believe this year will be the year that I am exonerated and pardoned. I'll keep you posted. Take care my friend. May the Great Spirit richly bless you. Sincerely, James.'

In February he wrote to me with further information about his case and mentioned that:

> 'Scott, I am waiting patiently for Mr Blackburn to file court papers in federal court. So far, things are looking very good. After February 22, 2006, there will probably be some media attention focused on my case. I will keep you posted on ongoing developments.'

As much as he enjoyed his job he was looking forward to five days of vacation. 'Too bad I can't go out and enjoy my vacation. I am locked down for 4 days.'

Nonetheless it gave him some time to rest and to concentrate on his case, even if he could not access the internet during this time. He was not even allowed to enter the lobby at his apartment, where the computer was located.

He was looking forward to the future and to having his pardon granted. He hoped that we would soon meet in order to celebrate together.

It was around this time that I was quite surprised to wake up one morning and switch on my phone to find an answerphone message. No one left answerphone messages on my phone during the middle of the night and as I listened I became even more surprised. It was Reyos who had called me in the early hours of the morning after he had finished work. He had not realized the great time difference between our countries and had thought I would be awake. His message was brief and he simply said he had called for a chat after seeing my phone number on a headed letter I had sent him. I returned the call and heard the phone ring. Eventually Reyos answered, sounding very tired and it was clear I had woken him up. He informed me he had tried calling straight after finishing work but had then gone to bed. He did not mind me waking him, however, and he was excited to speak with me. We spent a lot of time discussing accents, Reyos' work which he was finding very rewarding and his hopes of regaining his freedom.

It was during one of our phone chats that Reyos asked me to write a book about his case. I did not wish to do so at the time, being unfamiliar with the American justice system and Reyos seemed disappointed when I told him I was unable to. I also felt that a book would be unnecessary at that stage because Reyos' would receive his pardon and would have his named cleared. Little did I know at that time how even years later the campaign would still be ongoing and that there was indeed a need for such a book.

As February ended Reyos still waited for legal developments to overturn his conviction.

Whilst Reyos tried to fight his case through the Board of Pardons and Paroles, and through courts, there was another fight in his campaign for greater freedom. In May 2006 he began attempting to persuade the authorities to have a bulky monitoring device removed from around his waist. As a law abiding citizen he believes it is wrong he has to wear this heavy device which restricts his activities. In order to achieve his aim, a number of letters of support, acting as character references, were been sent to the authorities. Letters were sent by Donald L. Darling, Representatives Paul Moreno and Eddie Rodriguez and others, including myself. We wrote of Reyos' many positive attributes, including his intelligence, research, kind, caring and thoughtful character, honesty and professionalism. We also emphasized that Reyos worked and wanted to make an even greater contribution to society, which could only be achieved if he had greater freedom of movement.

In Darling's letter he wrote that:

'Extreme adversity often has extreme consequences. It can either build character, or destroy it. To paraphrase Emerson, "You gain the strength of the problems that you overcome." Adversity is no stranger to James Harry Reyos. I believe that James has responded to extreme adversity by allowing it to build character within himself. That is probably the best compliment/recommendation that I can give to anyone.'

Moreno's letter stated:

'This letter is in support of Mr. James Harry Reyos, which I have known and worked with regarding his defense for the past three years. I have found Mr. Reyos to be a pleasant and respectful gentleman. He has demonstrated honesty and concern for others. I have had numerous interactions with Mr. Reyos and find him to be quite articulate and intelligent. Through the interactions I have had with Mr. Reyos, I do not believe he is capable of committing the crime he was convicted of, to the contrary, I find Mr. Reyos to be kind hearted and genuinely concerned for the well being of others. He does not embody the profile of an individual who would commit a grievous crime like murder. Mr Reyos has my full support in his endeavors to clear his name and obtain the freedom he has been seeking for over twenty years.'

Rodriguez' letter stated:

'I have diligently reviewed documentation indicating his innocence and my office has contacted his parole officer to verify his good standing on supervision. My legislative staff has also had the opportunity to meet with Mr Reyos to discuss the facts of his case. Additionally, on the occasions Mr Reyos has visited my legislative office, he has always presented himself in a professional manner in both his appearance and demeanor.'

On May 15 he wrote me a letter, having spoken to me on the phone a little earlier. He told how much he loved the British accent and asked me lots of questions about Britain. He hoped to one day visit. He enclosed thirteen pages of information he wanted extracts of which adding to his website.

We were both very busy with work and campaigning. We exchanged some letters and several emails but little happened over the next few months as we waited, and waited, and became increasingly disappointed. By the end of 2006 there was no news regarding the legal battle to exonerate Reyos and the letters we wrote to have the bulky device removed went unanswered.

Doing OK

January 2007 was a quiet month in Reyos' campaign and I think the first time I heard from him was at the end of the month. On January 31 he sent me an email telling me he was 'doing ok.' He was pleased that American Justice was going to be airing their episode "Shamed Into Confession", which was about his case, on February 3.

There was no news regarding the Habeas Corpus writ, but as far as Reyos was concerned no news was not bad news:

> 'I have not heard from Mr Blackburn lately. However, I know he is still diligently working on the case. I continue to wait patiently for justice to prevail. It is a long wait, but I am patient and I know that it will eventually prevail.'

He added that he had been busier than usual with work, 'I am so sorry for not keeping in touch more often. I have been busy going to work, coming home, getting up in the morning, going to work. Work, work, work.'

In early March there was an update on the Habeas Corpus writ, but it was going to take some time yet, Reyos was told. It was in its 'final stages of being written and filed', Reyos told me on March 8, but original exhibits that were presented at trial were needed. I was unsure what exhibits these were, because all the forensic evidence had been destroyed, but assumed they were statements and crime scene photographs.

An associate of Jeff Blackburn's had informed Reyos of this development but had not given any timescale as to when the writ would be filed in federal court. 'I anticipate that within the next 2 to 4 months it will be ready to file.', Reyos wrote, expressing his hope and belief, adding:

> 'I continue to wait patiently for justice to prevail. This is the latest news, developments, concerning my progress for justice. It's my hope that the federal court of appeals will make a favorable and prompt ruling on the writ. Of course, the ONLY ruling that can be reached is to overturn my conviction based upon actual innocence.'

He was pleased that his website was receiving large numbers of visitors who were sending supportive messages.

He ended his message with his belief that 2007 would be the year he received justice, 'Hopefully, this year I will be able to return to my home state of New Mexico. I look forward to that very much.'

It was a busy period of time for me as the fight for Barry George's freedom hotted up, with the Criminal Cases Review Commission considering whether George's conviction should be referred to the Court of Appeal. It ultimately was, and he won his appeal in November 2007. Between March and May I fought an election campaign in my home town, as part of my political ambitions. However, I continued to make contact with Texan politicians and media to further promote Reyos' campaign in preparation for the writ of habeas corpus being filed.

Things were looking good, but in April 2007 a sad event took place which greatly distressed Reyos. That month Mike Lopez, one of Reyos' most loyal and influential supporters, died in a car accident. Reyos learnt the news a few weeks later, on May 9, when watching a televised legislative session which saw Rep Moreno giving a lengthy statement. Reyos went to the State Capitol to express his condolences and later told me how he felt he had lost a valued ally. 'Mr Lopez was the one who really got the ball rolling on my case by explaining the whole case to Rep Moreno.', he told me whilst adding that Lopez was, 'a man of great integrity.' This along with a delay in filing the habeas corpus caused Reyos great frustration and upset.

He believed that Lopez's legacy would live on and that Moreno would continue to pursue justice for Reyos.

Reyos' hope in March that the writ would be filed within two to four months was never realized and as the months passed it looked like it would not happen at all. Indeed despite receiving so many promises the writ was never filed. Other than A&E airing the episode on Reyos' case, in May that year, little of note took place on the campaign front.

With Reyos being busy at work our emails and letters became very infrequent until I had not heard from him for a number of months.

During September 2007 a friend of Reyos' contacted me expressing concern about him. I too was naturally concerned, having not heard from him for a few months. The friend told me that Reyos had phoned her on two occasions, during the spring, but had not been in touch since. She was worried he had had parole revoked and wanted to know if I had heard from him. I knew he had been upset by the death of Mike Lopez and frustrated by delays in his case. I sent a series of emails and letters, and tried to call, but heard nothing. In fact, if I remember right, his cell phone had been cut off. This made me seriously worry that he was indeed back in jail.

In the weeks that followed I tried to search online for information about Reyos' whereabouts and contacted Texan journalists who knew him. Nobody could manage to speak with him.

It was with the greatest of relief, therefore, that I received an email from him on December 11, 2007. His silence was based on him having been out of work and, no doubt, frustration with how slow his case was progressing. He wrote:

> 'Dear Scott: Hello! Hope you are fine. I am OK. I am currently job searching since I was layed off several months ago. So far, my case is slowly moving ahead. The investigation stage is over and now the writ is being put together. On November 18, 2007 the A&E tv network aired my case again, which coincided with the day of my arrest in 1982. I am wondering if they'll broadcast the case on December 21st, since that'll be the 26th anniversary of the crime. I am hoping they will. I would like to request that you contact people about the anniversary date. I will do the same here. This will be all for now. I will check my email in a few days for your reply. My best wishes to you Scott. Take care, -- James.'

I could now understand why I had not heard from Reyos for some time. I knew how much Reyos loved his work at the Mansion House. It was his pride and joy and gave him a sense of normality which had long been robbed of him during his years of imprisonment.

Two days later he emailed me again to talk about the weather, which was 'cold and rainy' in Austin and to tell me he had contacted some people about the upcoming anniversary of Father Ryan's murder. Reyos was relatively happy even if little appeared to be happening in his case.

The emails became less frequent as Reyos got another job which required him to work very long hours, with early starts, and his time on the Internet was therefore very restricted. Then the emails stopped altogether. At first I was not concerned because I believed he was busy and it was not unprecedented for him not to be in touch so regularly, but as the months passed without an email or a letter I was concerned, especially as I had always received a message at Christmas and New Year (even if the New Year message was belated). It was with great upset that I eventually discovered Reyos had been sent back to prison.

A Second Miscarriage of Justice

In 2008 a further development took place which saw what Reyos called a 'minor set back' in his fight for justice. By the summer of that year I had not heard from Reyos for quite some months and had become concerned about him. During that break in communication another supporter, who lives in the USA, had contacted me concerned about Reyos' health and wellbeing. He appeared to be depressed and weak from his ongoing battle to clear his name. It was not uncommon to not hear from him for several weeks on end, especially when he was working. His time on the Internet became extremely limited and because we lived on opposite sides of the world it was via the web that we usually communicated.

All my efforts to make contact with him were unsuccessful and I had almost given up hope of hearing from him again when unexpectedly I received an email in August from a woman whose name I will not reveal, to protect her identity:

'Hi,

I have a very difficult ethical dilemma. Several months back I was a victim of indecent exposure, while running in the dawn hours at Town Lake (while in Austin for a meeting). Yesterday I was served a subpoena from the Smith County Parole office. It is for a parole revocation hearing for James Harry Reyos. If I testify against him, he will go back to jail for a murder he did not commit. But I have to tell the truth. Please help!'

It would appear he was already in prison but that this situation would become more permanent depending upon the outcome of the hearing. That night I engaged in an email exchange with the woman, not knowing whether she was in fact genuine. I am regularly sent hoax emails in an attempt to discredit me or try and get a quote that can be used against me in the media or on an internet forum or blog. Unfortunately there are many people who are so angered by the prospect of an alleged killer being on the streets that they will do anything to try and have that alleged killer returned to prison, even if they have not troubled themselves to look into the circumstances of the case. It was some days later that I received confirmation, from a Texas journalist that Reyos was indeed up for a parole revocation hearing.

I explained to the woman that she should tell the truth and that if she had any doubts about it, that she should make those doubts clear at the hearing. Indeed she made it clear to me that she did have doubts: it was very dark, so dark in fact that the flasher was using a torch. The man was of Reyos' general appearance, she told me, but she had at no point in time identified him from a position where she could see him clearly, instead making a positive identification from a distance, without a line up of numerous suspects. Reyos looks fairly nondescript in appearance, though shorter than most men. He is a Native American but looks like many Native Americans or Mexicans. Further, she was given information by the police who informed her that Reyos was heavily under the influence of alcohol. This was worrying because it indicated she was being fed information by the police rather than her providing that information. The fact she made contact with me indicated she had been told the man's name. How can an eyewitness give an impartial testimony if she is given information by the police, including the man's name so much so that she carried out research about Reyos on the internet, locating his campaign website in the process, and saw photographs of him as a consequence? Even when seeing photographs she could not be sure that Reyos was the man who indecently exposed himself.

I told her in the strictest of terms that she must express her doubts at the hearing. I further mentioned to her that Reyos is a homosexual and therefore unlikely to flash at a woman no matter how drunk he was. He would gain no gratification from such an act. She agreed with me that Reyos may not have been the man she saw and pleasingly the ludicrous charge of indecent exposure was dismissed.

It made little difference, however. An email some days later from this same woman informed me that 'James is back in prison- parole was revoked.' It was difficult to get this confirmed, with me being on the other side of the world but a journalist in Texas checked for me and corroborated the story. I was astounded. I had learnt the female victim of the indecent exposure had retracted her allegation against Reyos. It appeared to me that the authorities in Texas do not care if something is retracted, just like Reyos' retraction of his false confession.

In fact it was not until September 16, 2009 that I actually heard directly from Reyos who wrote to me as prisoner #359384 from Hughes Unit in Gatesville, Texas. He had contacted me via one of his supporters in the USA at the beginning of that month but I had sent word back to him that I needed to hear from him directly.

His letter clearly showed an increased amount of stress and frustration to what I was accustomed to. The usual politeness was present but there were clear undertones of anger. He explained to me that when he was returned to prison he did not have my contact details, or indeed the contact details of anyone he communicated with, and so he had struggled to make contact with me. I had been unable to make contact for a long period of time because he was transferred between prisons and it was difficult to trace him. He told me:

> 'I am sitting here in my cell writing this letter. I still can't believe it was 18 (eighteen) months ago that I was arrested – falsely arrested! – and charged – falsely charged! – with the misdemeanor Indecent Exposure. Even though the charge was officially dismissed by the presiding judge, I was subsequently revoked on parole and sent back to prison. I am going through another miscarriage of justice.'

He outlined the details of what had happened on Friday April 25, 2008 and protested his innocence again of both the charge of indecent exposure and the murder of Father Patrick Ryan. 'I have been honest with you, Scott: I know I am innocent in the murder of Father Patrick Ryan! – and I know I am innocent in the indecent exposure case!!', he told me.

My email exchange with the victim of the indecent exposure had already been sufficient for me to have serious doubts that Reyos was the perpetrator in that case and I was, of course, convinced of his innocence in the Father Ryan murder. He was clearly concerned that I would cease my support for him and I wrote to assure him this would not be the case. Reyos provided me with further details of his account of events on that April morning.

According to his account during the early hours of Friday April 25, 2008 Reyos was on his way to work, walking down the sidewalk towards a bus stop from which he would catch his usual bus, when a police car stopped beside him. Confused but curious Reyos was soon terrified when the officer told him he matched the description of a man who had indecently exposed himself to a female who had been jogging in the area. "You got to be kidding. I committed no such offence!", Reyos exclaimed but it left no impression on the officer who promptly cuffed him and placed him in the back of the police car. The vehicle was then driven to a nearby spot where the alleged victim was parked in her car. It was still dark by this time as the police car pulled up in front of the jogger. The officer approached the jogger's vehicle before returning to Reyos and instructed him to get out and stand at the rear of the police car. The jogger's headlights were shone on him at full beam and within a few moments Reyos was told "she has identified you." He was arrested and charged with indecent exposure.

The woman who made the allegation of indecent exposure failed to attend a formal court hearing for trial by judge and so a new hearing was organized. Again the victim refused to appear in court for a trial by jury and so charges were dropped against Reyos. Reyos thought his problems were now over. He told me: 'I thought I was going to be released from jail. I was very happy to think that I was going home, going back to work, and continuing on parole.' It was not to be.

Despite the charge having been dismissed a parole revocation hearing took place because Reyos had been arrested, even though he was not convicted of any offence. This time the victim made an appearance. She entered the small court room, was sworn in and sat approximately five feet from Reyos. It was the first time she had seen him close up. She was then asked, in the light of the day, "Is this the man you saw expose himself to you?" She hesitated for a few moments, looked at Reyos and replied, "I am not sure. The guy was taller."

Again, Reyos had good grounds for optimism but after having been wrongly convicted of Father Patrick Ryan's murder, despite a strong alibi, he should have realized that justice was unlikely to work for him. Despite the parole hearing officer's recommendation to not revoke parole, the Board of Pardons and Paroles decided that Reyos had committed a misdemeanor, posed a danger to society and should therefore be sent straight back to prison to continue his sentence for murder. In doing so the Board of Pardons and Paroles disregarded the entire lack of evidence against Reyos in relation to the indecent exposure, just as his trial jury had disregarded the lack of evidence against him for murder.

Reyos' account to me continued:

> 'If I was not a parolee, not on parole whatsoever, when the charge was dismissed by the judge, I would have walked scot-free. But just because I am a parolee, I am in prison again. This is all because a woman "misidentified" me as the perpetrator – even after the court "officially" dismissed the charge – and even after the complaining witness failed to identify me in a face-to-face hearing.'

The consequence of such a flawed decision by the Board of Pardons and Paroles were his immediate imprisonment and this angered Reyos tremendously:

> 'Scott, I lost my job, my apartment – and my freedom again! – because of this lady who misidentified me. If only she would have told the policeman that earlier morning when asked to identify the perpetrator, "I am not sure. The guy was taller." I would not be in prison again because I would have never been arrested. This lady is going about her daily life with no concern that she destroyed a man's – an innocent man's! – life. <u>Misidentifications</u> lead to many wrongful convictions … and sadly, to parole revocations! Scott, I greatly appreciate your not giving up on me and my fight for justice. I know in my heart that I am truly innocent of the murder of Father Patrick Ryan. I DID NOT KILL FATHER RYAN!! I will always profess my innocence. Scott, thank you for your full support.'

He was frustrated not to have heard from Attorney Jeff Blackburn but believed he was still working on the case. Reyos was worried I would close the campaign, which he recognized as the only way of directly informing supporters of his plight and, along with the often repeated documentary, the main means of keeping the message of his innocence alive. He urged me to keep the site live, telling me:

> 'To close it will only hide the truth of my innocence, and will hide the wrongs of the Texas criminal justice system. I have been honest with you, Scott: I know I am innocent in the murder of Father Patrick Ryan! – and I know I am innocent in the indecent exposure case!!'

I had been considering taking a step back from the campaign because I had not heard from Reyos. I had never doubted his innocence but was unsure what could be done for his campaign. I had also been informed (wrongly as it happened) that there was more to the parole revocation than the wrongful indecent exposure charge. However, Reyos' letter ended such foolhardy concerns I may have had.

He continued:

> 'Sure, I am going through a minor set back in my fight for justice but I will NEVER give up trying to clear my name. As you know there are many supporters backing me. We must all continue to fight, to see justice prevail. The fight for justice is not only for me, it's for Father Ryan too, to see that his killer is brought to justice.'

It was typical of Reyos to play down the struggles he faced. Being back in prison was more than just a 'minor set back'.

Speaking of the campaign to clear his name of the murder charge, Reyos told me:

> 'I still believe that the Boise "John Doe" is linked to the crime. There has to be a way to identify him, especially now with the fingerprints and photo of him. Once his identity is known, the backtracking into his past can begin. "Who is he?", is the $64000 question. Governor Rick Perry is up for re-election next November 2010. My wrongful conviction needs to be brought to his attention, put before him. He must act to correct this injustice. He can't always give me the deaf ear. I am truly innocent – my case demands nothing less than a Full Pardon

Based Upon Innocence. I am going to make my wrongful conviction a cause celebre. Thank you for your support, Scott.'

I will outline here the Parole Revocation Process because it is very relevant in understanding what Reyos experienced.

When a parole officer believes the terms of parole have been violated they submit a report to the Parole Division. The Parole Division then reviews the report to determine whether there is sufficient evidence to indicate parole conditions have been breached and whether a warrant should be issued to detain the parolee pending an administrative hearing.

Once the parolee has been detained on the warrant the Parole Division decides whether a hearing should take place. If the violation involves a criminal charge then the Parole Division will defer the parole revocation process pending the outcome of those criminal charges.

Once a revocation hearing is organized the parolee is interviewed by a parole officer and advised of their legal rights during the revocation hearing process.

Hearings are conducted by both parole officers and supervisory personnel from the Parole Division.

The first phase of the hearing is where the allegation is made and evidence is presented which indicates the conditions of parole have been violated. If sufficient evidence of a violation is presented then it progresses to the adjustment phase of proceedings, usually known as a mitigation hearing, where issues such as the offender's work history, compliance with drug treatment programs (where applicable), adherence to conditions of release and previous violations of parole.

If, upon the conclusion of these two stages of hearing, it is found there is evidence to show that parole has been violated then a revocation hearing is called. The decision is made by a Board Panel consisting of three members. Alternatives to a revocation hearing can include: transfer to a Substance Abuse Felony Punishment Facility; the option to not revoke parole but allow parole under supervision; allow continued parole but with modification to conditions of parole.

If the Board makes the decision to revoke parole, as in Reyos' case, the parolee receives a written report by the hearing officer which sets out the justification for revocation. It is possible, in certain circumstances, for the offender to request the Board reopens the revocation hearing in order to appeal the decision.

Reyos wrote to me again in December 2009. His letter was accompanied by a Christmas card showing the Virgin Mary holding the baby Jesus, in which he expressed his hope for peace on Earth. Although Reyos is a Native American, and does not adhere to any Christian faith, I have received a number of Christmas cards from him over the years and he has always gained some pleasure and hope from the season of goodwill.

At this time he was particularly hopeful because another case in Texas, where two men (Claude Simmons and Christopher Scott) had been wrongly convicted of murder, had had their convictions overturned after twelve years of imprisonment because the real killer had come forward and confessed. He was frustrated, however, because he had not heard anything from Jeff Blackburn, any of his family and had only heard from one other supporter. 'So perhaps, you are the only friend – and supporter in my fight for justice- now'. It was a melancholy note, at odds with his usual joy in the face of adversity. He added, in clear frustration:

> 'On Monday, December 21, 2009 will mark the 28th anniversary of Father Ryan's murder. After 28 years, the REAL KILLER is still roaming free while I am serving time in prison for his crime.'

He asked about a photo of him in a Walgreens wearing a green plaid shirt and red t shirt 'smiling real big.' He thought he had sent me the photograph but I had never seen it.

> 'I believe that picture captures my true identity: a very easygoing and happy person. Despite my wrongful conviction, I am still a happy person, not allowing life's setbacks to get me down.'

His letter ended:

> 'I will keep you apprised of any developments concerning my case. I still greatly appreciate your full support in my fight for

justice. I'll never lose hope that some day I will be exonerated, and pardoned. Thank you, Scott, for everything. May the Great Spirit richly bless you during the Holiday Season. May the New Year, 2010, be a Happy and Prosperous one for you. Sincerely, James Harry Reyos.'

We exchanged a few letters in early 2010 but being in prison, and having other people to contact, Reyos struggled to write as much as he would have liked to have done.

On May 4, 2010 Reyos wrote to me to tell me he was 'doing fine' and stating he would soon be up before the Board of Pardons and Paroles to be given consideration for parole and that he would be informed of a decision within two to three months. He told me he was looking forward to being released so that he could rebuild his life once again. He was wanting to return to Austin and had been told by his former landlord that he could return to his old apartment. He was encouraged by the case of Frank Sterling who had been exonerated just weeks earlier after nineteen years of serving a sentence in New York for a murder which DNA had proven he had not committed. He was, however, frustrated to have still not heard from Jeff Blackburn who he had long considered to be his main hope of clearing his name.

I continued to write to the Board of Pardons and Paroles on many occasions providing evidence that the jogger had been wrong in her identification. I received no response and I was immensely angered that the authorities in Texas could blatantly ignore what was clear proof that they had locked up an innocent man.

In fact I wrote to the Board of Pardons and Paroles on many, many occasions, expressing my full support for Reyos, commending him for his caring personality and outlining yet again the evidence showing that the victim of the indecent exposure did not believe Reyos was the man she saw. His former landlord had also written to the Board, confirming that Reyos had accommodation if he was released.

I also again wrote to Governor Rick Perry pointing out that parole should not have been revoked, on evidential grounds that the woman was mistaken in her identification.

Such is the regard for justice in Texas that the Governor (an elected politician rather than a legal expert), who has the power to grant pardons and paroles for inmates, failed to even acknowledge written statements which cast immense doubt upon the correctness of the decision to revoke parole.

I repeated my pleas to other Texan politicians and urged other supporters to call for Reyos' release. My efforts, and those of the few supporters who tried to help, were ignored. I could not believe that there was evidence Reyos had done no wrong, and so parole was unjustly revoked, yet the authorities completely ignored me.

The authorities do not seem to care that the victim had stated, without any prompting, that she was uncertain in her identification and believed that Reyos was probably not the culprit. Documents were sent to Perry but two years on they had not been acted upon. Given such a reluctance to accept a mistake over a charge of indecent exposure it is hardly surprising the authorities refuse to investigate the probability that Reyos was wrongly convicted of Father Ryan's murder.

Soon later I heard rumors that Reyos had been granted parole and was free but my hopes were dashed when I learnt there was no truth in them. James Harry Reyos was still in cell 30 of building 3-C-2 of the Alfred Hughes Unit. The Board of Pardons and Paroles had rejected the irrefutable evidence, and Reyos' good character, and turned down his request to be released on parole. Reyos had to spend yet another Christmas behind bars, but this time for two crimes he had not committed.

Shortly before Christmas in 2010 I received a Christmas card from him which included the words 'I am still fighting for JUSTICE'. I wondered how much longer would that fight last?

The Walk to Freedom

As 2011 began there were renewed efforts to ensure Reyos' release from prison, on parole. If we could ensure his release on parole we could then concentrate on his exoneration.

With my representations to the Board of Pardons and Paroles and to Governor Rick Perry falling on deaf ears, despite the strength of my arguments, I turned to the media.

I renewed appeals for information regarding the identity of the man who committed suicide in Boise in 1982. If the man's identity could be established it would theoretically be possible to determine his movements at around the time of the murder of Father Patrick Ryan. We could possibly work out whether he might potentially have been involved in the murder or whether we were wasting our time and energy in considering that possibility.

I gave interviews to a television station in Boise, recording my voice online and providing lots of information about the Boise Doe and about Reyos' case. I urged people to get in touch with me if they thought they might know the identity of the mystery man.

A news story was aired but I was disappointed that Reyos' campaign was not referred to and that the appeal for information was not used. Whilst it was great the story was publicized on television, I have always found that potential witnesses are more willing to speak to people like me than they are to speak to the police. Some people do not trust the police, or they feel their information might not be important enough, and so they do not make contact. Whereas people are more willing to make contact with me because I have no connection to the authorities and because if the information is not of particular interest it is only my time that has been taken up, rather than time which could be spent looking for criminals. So I was more than a little annoyed that the campaign's contact details were not mentioned.

I promoted the case through social media, setting up a campaign group which attracted lots of new campaigners. I urged these people to contact their local politicians and to lobby Governor Perry. Some of the members did, but most chose not to.

A student journalist wrote an excellent feature which generated interest from her fellow students.

The documentary on Reyos' case was again broadcast and people from England, the Republic of Ireland, South America and Australia got in touch, as well as people from the USA.

Across the world people were able to see Reyos is innocent, but the Texan authorities were blind to this double miscarriage of justice.

I continued to contact Jeff Blackburn in the hope he might once again try to help Reyos, even if only to enable him to obtain parole. In June 2010 I finally heard from him:

> 'Hey Scott Great to hear from you. I have owed James Harry a long letter for a good while now. I will get one to him this week. I believe with all my heart that he is innocent and that he needs to be out. Getting that done is another story altogether of course. There is a small possibility that we could get him out using a "junk science" angle no one has tried before.'

In a further email that day he added, 'I will write to James this weekend. Thanks for looking after him and thanks for being so patient.' Unfortunately it was the last time we would hear from him.

'Happy New Year 2011!', Reyos wrote in his first letter of the year, 'I hope and pray that your New Year is prosperous and enjoyable. My New Year is beginning on the happy side.'

He went on to explain that the Wesleyan Innocence Project had contacted him before Christmas sending a lengthy questionnaire enquiring about the facts of his case and informed him that they were 'preparing to commence a preliminary investigation' into his case. The WIP had been established in 2005 and was comprised of law students, working under the direction of a qualified attorney, to research cases of alleged miscarriage of justice in Texas and determine whether there were grounds to launch an appeal. It claimed to be the largest student run innocence project in the world. Although they were only students they brought fresh eyes to the case and renewed hope. In a number of cases innocence projects across the USA, and elsewhere in the world, have achieved some success. He added:

> 'After reviewing the questionnaire, they'll write to me to apprise me of their decision to pursue my wrongful conviction.

I'll wait patiently for their decision. ... Perhaps WIP can help me right the injustice I am going through.'

Reyos wrote them a substantial letter answering all of their questions in detail. It was his usual style and I would expect nothing less from him. However, the students never received the letter. I suspected that the prison had disposed of it as part of their censorship.

In the absence of Jeff Blackburn the students offered Reyos the only form of legal representation he had. It was therefore disappointing that after a few months they ceased to show interest in Reyos' case.

I asked them why they had ceased to be interested and was informed they could not be involved because they had yet to receive information from Reyos even though he had sent them a number of letters. I carried on trying to get them involved, but to no avail.

Meanwhile Reyos remained optimistic that he would be granted parole once again. He informed me in early 2011 that he was coming up for parole consideration in June and that he was confident of his chances.

June arrived, and passed, and Reyos was not successful in his bid for parole. I was disgusted that with such overwhelming evidence that Reyos was innocent of the indecent exposure charge that he should still be languishing in jail. Being on the other side of the world there was so little I could do other than continue to write letters to the authorities, continue to raise Reyos' profile in the media and urge his supporters in the USA to write to their politicians.

One of the main targets of my letters and emails was, of course, the then Governor of Texas, Rick Perry. So I was very surprised to learn that Perry was campaigning to be selected the Republican Party candidate to take on Barack Obama for the White House. At that time Perry was the longest serving Governor of the state of Texas.

I started a letter writing campaign at this time, urging the Governor to intervene and using his presidential ambitions to persuade him to do the right thing. A few supporters in the USA joined in. I launched a letter writing campaign involving Reyos' supporters. Despite me contacting more than 200 of his supporters, by email and through Facebook, asking for five minutes of their time, only three people offered to help. Still, it was useful to have people living in the USA contacting Perry and their own State politicians. Our efforts failed to result in a single response from the then Governor, however.

Early in 2012 Perry abandoned his presidential ambitions but we continued writing to him and urging him to do the right thing by Reyos.

It was around this time that I received an email from Reyos' email account. I was amazed and relieved and hoped that he had been released. However, upon opening the email I became despondent once more because I soon realized it was a spam message and that his email account had been hacked.

Towards the end of 2011, shortly before my wedding, a photograph was given to me by my parents. The photograph was of a little baby; me. The photograph dates to 1983 and shows me aged only a few months, unable to even stand. Although I have often thought about the longevity of Reyos' plight, it hit me once again when I viewed this photograph. The photograph was taken at a time when Reyos was in prison. I am unsure exactly what month the photograph was taken but Reyos was either awaiting his trial or he had been convicted. There I was as a tiny baby and as I looked at the photograph, with Reyos still in prison, I was 6'1" in height, 29 years old, my hair thinning and even (according to my wife) some signs of grey hair. During the period since the photograph was taken I had learnt to talk, learnt to walk, learnt to read and write, gone to school, traveled to many countries, gone to university, traveled around some more countries, had relationships, settled down ready to get married, got jobs and experienced periods of unemployment. So much has changed for me since 1983 in what is literally a lifetime. Yet ever since that little baby stared into the camera Reyos has been experiencing the same nightmare day in, day out. He has been waking up with the knowledge he is held responsible for a horrifically violent murder and he has been fighting to clear his name. That has been the focus of his days since the photograph was taken. That photograph, and the thoughts I have just outlined, are what keeps me motivated to campaign for Reyos.

I received a Christmas card from Reyos that year but there was no letter. I remain convinced Reyos was being banned, by the prison authorities, from writing anything about his conditions or his case. It is most unlike him to not write anything other than a simple note on the card expressing his hope and belief that 2012 would see his release. I suspect he did write a letter but the prison staff removed it.

As 2012 began I continued to write emails, and letters, to the Board of Pardons and Paroles and to Governor Perry, as well as to other Texan politicians. I also continued to try and encourage other supporters to write to their State Representatives and Governor Perry but very few did. I was always amazed how many people offered to help but when I asked them to do a five minute job only a few of them actually bothered. Everyone could see that a miscarriage of justice had taken place but there were too many who wanted to do nothing about it. I am frequently reminded of the words spoken by the Civil Rights activist Dr Martin Luther King, Jr, "Injustice anywhere is a threat to justice everywhere". I am further reminded of the following poem about the Holocaust:

> 'First they came for the Socialists and I did not speak out – Because I was not a Socialist
> Then they came for the Trade Unionists, and I did not speak out – Because I was not a Trade Unionist
> Then they came for the Jews, and I did not speak out – Because I was not a Jew
> Then they came for me – and there was no one left to speak for me.'

Sure, Reyos' plight was very different to those imprisoned, and murdered, by the Nazi regime. However, the principle is similar because Reyos was in prison due to a flawed system which can only be challenged if people have the courage to speak up against it.

I again wrote to Jeff Blackburn and received no response, and as ever I wrote to politicians but received no acknowledgements, let alone full replies. Meanwhile Reyos continued to languish in a Texas jail cell.

I wrote to the Jicarilla Apache Nation and obtained some support from one of the younger members of the tribe who assured me he would help by putting pressure on the new tribal leaders when they were elected. I was informed the tribal leaders had considerable influence. I could only hope they would put pressure on the Board of Pardons and Paroles to release Reyos on parole so that he could continue to fight to clear his name. I also wrote to the tribal leaders despite being unfamiliar with the correct procedure of writing to them and the correct salutations and so forth. I hoped that my letter and the efforts of the young member of the tribe would help.

I wrote to Reyos' supporters among the Texas State Representatives. Representative Eddie Rodriguez responded, thanking me for contacting him. He informed me he had contacted the Texas Department of Criminal Justice asking them to look into my 'allegations' regarding the unreliability of the evidence used to revoke parole and that I should contact the prosecuting attorney if I had any evidence. I was a little disappointed because I know Rodriquez supports Reyos, so I had hoped for him to do more than just write a letter to the Department of Criminal Justice. In fairness to him he had limited influence but I had hoped for more.

In the meantime I was concerned that Reyos was being prevented from having access to the outside world. He was not responding to my letters and others, who I knew he had written to some time previously had not received the letters which I knew had been sent.

On July 1, 2012 I finally received a letter from him. He had stuck stamps on the envelope showing the American flag with the words' JUSTICE FOREVER' written beneath the flag. I wondered how Reyos felt about the American flag and the American views of 'justice forever', being a member of a tribe displaced by American settlers and forced to live in a reservation before being convicted under the American justice system for a crime he had not committed.

In his letter he sounded very upbeat:

> 'Thank you for continuing to be a "strong supporter" of mine. I know it's a long, uphill battle to obtain JUSTICE; I will never lose hope that someday it will happen. We just need to contact the right people to help move this miscarriage of justice forward to a successful end. I will continue to work diligently on my case to get the ultimate resolution: Exoneration, and Full Pardon Based Upon Innocence.'

The reason for his happier tone soon became apparent. He went on to tell me some excellent news:

> 'Scott, I have some good news to convey to you: I have been GRANTED PAROLE. Enclosed is a "Reproduced Verbatim

Copy From Original" of the Texas Board of Pardons and Paroles' NOTICE OF PAROLE PANEL DECISION.'

Sure enough enclosed was the text of the decision which read, 'After a review of your case, the Board of Pardons and Paroles decision is to grant you parole during the month/year you become eligible.' He was granted parole on condition that restrictions were imposed on his consumption of alcohol and drugs and that he continued to undergo treatment for alcohol addictions. It continued:

> 'The Institutional Division will monitor your treatment plan progress and will report your progress to the Board of Pardons and Paroles. This decision may be changed by the Board if there is a change in your status or classification or if additional information is received.'

Parole guidelines have changed significantly since Reyos was convicted, in particular as a result of too many people being granted parole. In deciding whether or not to grant parole the Board had to consider the following: Reyos' age upon entering prison; his history of supervisory release revocations for felony offenses; prior incarcerations; employment history; the offence for which he was convicted; Reyos' age at the time of being considered for parole; whether Reyos was a gang member; Reyos' education and training programs completed during the present incarceration; his disciplinary conduct; his prison custody level.

By considering all of the above, the Board were able to assess Reyos as being low risk to the public and they decided to grant parole.

The timing of the letter had been perfect, as Reyos told me. 'The Board's decision to grant parole was made on 05/25/2012 (a coincidence that it was on my birthday – I guess I couldn't have asked for a better birthday present!)'. He told me he intended to return to Austin, to the same complex he had lived in prior to parole being revoked in 2008. He had not shared the wonderful news with me previously because he had not known exactly when he would be released although he believed it would be in July. 'I am very happy to be leaving prison soon.', he told me. It was a classic comment. Reyos is an emotional man but he always tries to keep a level head. I had no doubt he was ecstatic about being released even though it would mean freedom only in a limited sense of the word. He would return to a small apartment which he would not be allowed to leave in the evenings, weekends of on public holidays. He would have a bulky monitoring device around his person at all times. He would have to schedule all of his movements and gain approval for them from his probation officer. And of course he would still remain a convicted murderer who could be returned to prison at any time if the justice system desired it.

He was pleased with the campaign update that I gave him, regarding the popularity of his website and he told me he was working on a list of people for me to contact to help raise further awareness of his case. 'Many people badly need to see the gross miscarriage of justice that I am going through.'

He shared my concerns about the lack of contact from Jeff Blackburn and he acknowledged for the first time that Blackburn had lost interest in his case:

> 'Since I have returned to prison (since April 2008), I have not received one letter from Mr Blackburn, even though I have written him numerous times, have asked my penpal Brenda to email him a few times, and your own emails to him. All to no avail. No replies. So that should tell us that he obviously does not want to pursue my case any further. I have no plans, at this time, to contact Mr Blackburn.'

Although Blackburn has not been in touch with Reyos or myself since 2010, he has spoken to the media about Reyos' case much more recently, and we are therefore sure that he still believes in Reyos' innocence. No doubt he is busy working on other cases but we hope his belief in Reyos continues and we would welcome his involvement in the case in the future.

Reyos accepted the difficulties he faced. For a long time he had believed that by gaining public support he could overturn his conviction. Now he acknowledged (I am sure he had long privately known) that he needed much more than that:

> 'In my case there is clear and convincing evidence PROVING my innocence but, yet, because there is NO available DNA

(which will make it easier for the case to be overturned), it makes it harder to obtain justice, to get me exonerated and pardoned. ... There continues to be exonerations happening here in Texas. I read about them every so often in the newspapers. Again, all involve DNA testing that subsequently proves the defendant is actually innocent. While those people who are ACTUALLY INNOCENT – with NO available DNA (like me!) sit in prison, can't get justice, can't get the courts to look at our claims of innocence, are forgotten. My case is definitely a poster-case for a wrongful conviction, a miscarriage of justice.'

It is a frustrating situation. Where there is no DNA because none was left at the crime scene or because it was contaminated or destroyed by incompetent, inexperienced or unprofessional police forces, how does an innocent person prove their innocence? This is especially a problem after many years have elapsed because any potential witnesses who did not come forward at the time but who may be able to support an alibi or cast doubt on an identification will be scrutinized with tremendous intensity to establish whether they are reliable. Other witnesses, who did come forward at the time but who might be able to provide additional information to that given in their original evidence, will not be believed because of the passage of time. Short of a confession from the real culprit it was difficult to see how Reyos could have his case overturned. Doubt was not enough. There had always been doubts about the evidence against him but the justice system had not cared at any point in time. Reyos had always known this, but he had still maintained some faith in the system that had already robbed him of more than half his life.

He was thankful for all my help, and the help of other supporters:

'Thank you for all that you are doing for me, even though you are way over on the other side of the world. I wish you lived in the United States. Nonetheless, I am truly thankful for your continued support. May the Great Spirit richly bless you.'

I knew that so little could be done by me although I will continue to do all that I can for him. I am unsure what influence the campaign had on helping secure Reyos' release on parole but I like to think that the letters I wrote, and the letters from other supporters, may have played some role. I believe discreet words were probably had by the leaders of the Jicarilla tribe to the authorities in Texas and so I suspect my efforts had some impact but it was the culmination of many efforts and prolonged campaigning by Reyos himself that the authorities allowed Reyos' release, even if they were completely unwilling to acknowledge they had done anything wrong.

As much as I wanted to meet Reyos I did not wish I was in the United States. I did, however, wish that Reyos was living in Britain. Despite its monumental flaws, at least if the British concept of justice was applied to his case he might potentially have had a good chance of gaining an appeal against his conviction because although politics is involved in many high profile criminal cases in Britain, it is not ultimately a single politician who can play a significant role in deciding upon a person's fate.

I thought parole might be too good to be true or that perhaps Reyos had got his dates wrong, but Reyos does not make mistakes when it comes to facts and figures. His organization skills have always amazed me. I had always believed that he was not eligible for parole until July 2013, not July 2012. I checked online via the Texas Department of Criminal Justice and was relived to see that Reyos was indeed to be paroled on July 17.

He wrote to me again a few days later to send me the list of people to contact which he had promised. It only involved contacting 76 emails to organizations and individuals. I was used to him requesting to contact many more than this number. He wrote:

> 'Hello again. I hope and pray y'all are doing fine. For me (as of this dated letter) I am still waiting patiently – but anxious at the same time: understandable – for my release. As I get closer to the end of July, the CLOSER I get to release. By the time you receive this letter, I might have already been released.'

I was furious that the whole world could quite easily find out that Reyos was due to be released on July 17 but that the man himself had been left entirely in the dark about his release date. Despite having been granted parole he had been forced to endure the added punishment of not being able to fully psychologically prepare himself for that day when he could walk free. It was a petty move on the part of the Texas justice system and completely unnecessary.

He hoped that by contacting all of the 76 people and organizations that further awareness would be raised of the case. He hoped it would specifically:

> 'get people to ask – despite the overwhelming, substantial and CREDIBLE evidence "PROVING" my innocence – why I have not been accorded due process of the law; why I have not been exonerated and pardoned yet, based upon ACTUAL innocence. With two prosecutors speaking out on my behalf (former prosecutor Dennis Cadra, and current DA John W. Smith), why do the top Texas officials continue to deny me JUSTICE?'

He told me he did still have faith in the US justice system, and the Texas state system, and seemed more upbeat than in previous letters but I suspected he was trying to put a brave face on the situation. I really needed to speak to him at length and I was looking forward to his release so that we could discuss the case and the campaign in more detail. I was eager to see how he was and how he felt about his situation.

Later in July I received a card, dated Sunday July 15, 2012. Reyos sent me the card thanking me for my friendship and support. It was typical of Reyos' caring and warm nature. His handwriting was very neat, as always, but it was slightly different. The amateur graphologist in me detected that there was more than a little degree of excitement and it was soon obvious why this was the case. I read the card:

> 'Scott – As of tomorrow, Monday July 16, 2012, I will be leaving the Texas prison system. I'll write to you when I get to Austin.
>
> I will soon be able to do more on my case – my ultimate goal is Exoneration and FULL PARDON BASED UPON ACTUAL INNOCENCE.
>
> Thank you for being a strong supporter of mine.
>
> May the Great Spirit richly bless you!
>
> Thank you, Scott, for all that you've done for me. I am truly grateful.'

I was amazed because according to the Texas Department of Criminal Justice website, Reyos had been scheduled for release on Tuesday 17 July and there was a note saying that this was subject to change. Based on my experience in other cases in my own country of Great Britain I was expecting there to be delays. Even upon receiving Reyos' card I had felt it necessary to check that he had in fact been released and I was glad to see that when I typed his name in the TDCJ offender locator search engine I was told there were no prisoners of that name in any Texas prison.

It was an anxious wait for me to hear from him. I knew he had been released on Monday July 16, but when I had not heard from him again a week and a half later I became concerned. Could he have suffered a breakdown from not being sufficiently prepared to re-enter ordinary society? Of course he had only been in prison for four years but I was worried he may have found returning to Austin to be too emotional and stressful. I knew he would not be able to get online for at least a few weeks, and that he would need time to settle in his new surroundings, and that he might not have money to pay for stamps, but I expected to hear something from him.

As July came to an end I had still not heard from Reyos. August followed suit, as did another five months.

It was not until January 2013 that I heard, through a friend of his, that Reyos was okay. He had only just found the strength to begin to resume as ordinary a life as he could having struggled for several months to cope with once again being released. He had returned to the same apartment block where he had lived before his parole was so wrongly and so cruelly taken from him. His landlord, who had been a long term supporter, had kindly kept all of his belongings in storage. He did not yet have a job but he was 'doing well' I was told.

I heard little from Reyos until October 2013. He had been attempting to rebuild his life and so, quite understandably, he had been busy. I received an email on Halloween 'I'm still fighting this wrongful conviction. Hope some action is taken soon – before Governor Rick Perry leaves office next year. JUSTICE must prevail soon.', he told me.

Elusive Justice

The year 2014 began in the same way that every year had begun for Reyos, since 1983 when he spent his first New Year fighting to clear his name.

On January 2, 2014 I received an email from him. Having been a public holiday Reyos was prevented from leaving his apartment on New Year's Day itself, so he had no access to the internet.

'HAPPY NEW YEAR 2014!!!', his email opened, before continuing:

> 'Scott, I pray that 2014 will be prosperous for you. I hope that you enjoy all the success that you want. Thanks for all that you do for the WRONGFULLY CONVICTED. You are commended for all your efforts to seeing "justice" prevail. "Justice" is very elusive, however, if you want to attain it, you keep fighting for it, toward it. If you are truly innocent – ACTUALLY innocent – of the crime, just like in my case, you keep fighting for justice. Sure, it's an uphill battle against a corrupt system of justice but you keep fighting – because you know in your heart you are ACTUALLY innocent. "JUSTICE" must prevail at some point. Thanks, Scott. As always, my best: JAMES.'

Despite recognizing that justice was so very elusive, Reyos began the year optimistic. Enjoying the cold weather, and wishing it could be cold all year round, he told me he was 'doing well, staying strong, HOPEFUL that justice will someday prevail for me.', adding, 'I'm blessed to have a friend and true supporter (like you, Scott) on my side. Together we'll fight to the end....and then some more to obtain JUSTICE.'

The cold weather was not the only source of some joy for Reyos. In February 2014 he sent me a video relating to the cases of two men who had been exonerated. As always, seeing others clear their names for crimes they had not committed reinforced his belief that his conviction could also be overturned.

It is hard to maintain a faith in a system that repeatedly fails, and which fails to even fully consider claims of innocence such as

Reyos'. At this time Reyos was hooked on a Sunday night program on CNN called 'Death Row Stories'. He was moved by the stories of people facing execution and was grateful that despite the difficulties he faced, he had not had to experience the prospect of execution in the name of justice. 'SHAME on the American justice system that it continuously convicts INNOCENT people.', he wrote to me having just watched one of the episodes.

Little else of note happened in 2014 as Reyos continued to try and rebuild his life, with attempts to clear his name temporarily taking a back seat. I became a father in this year and so I was also too busy to do as much as I would have liked for Reyos, but he seemed to be rebuilding his life. As the year came towards its end, the 33rd anniversary of Father Ryan's murder arrived and caused Reyos to reflect, as he had countless times over the decades, on the course of events:

> 'Scott, I am here in my tiny room reflecting upon 33 years ago, which marks the very day that Father Patrick Ryan was brutally murdered in an Odessa, Texas motel room. As you well know, Scott, I AM TRULY – COMPLETELY - and FACTUALLY innocent of this crime. I hope that J-U-S-T-I-C-E will prevail for me soon. That's my only hope. Thank you, Scott, for being a strong, unwavering, and dedicated supporter of mine. Happy Holidays, and prosperous New Year 2015.'

As with 2014, little happened in 2015, apart from Rick Perry leaving the office of State Governor. His successor was Greg Abbott and so letters and emails were sent to Governor Abbott but, as with his predecessor, there were no responses. It seemed Abbott cared no more about justice than Perry. We continued to try and put pressure on the authorities but our appeals continued to fall on death ears.

Reyos sent me many news stories about other cases where convictions had been overturned, often on the basis of new scientific techniques proving that the individuals convicted of murder were innocent. The fact convictions were being overturned, and pardons granted, continued to give Reyos hope but it was different in his case. Had the forensic evidence in his case not been destroyed even technology available 20 years ago would have proved someone else had killed Father Ryan.

Reyos was particularly pleased to learn that Michael McAlister had been cleared, in May 2015, having spent 29 years in prison as a result of a mistaken identity. However, again, there were no witnesses who claimed to see Reyos commit the murder. So there was no mistaken identity to argue about.

The only way to prove Reyos' innocence was to find the real killer and that seemed impossible and could never be proven, without forensic evidence, unless the real killer confessed, which seemed unlikely to happen. The best we could hope for was that the Governor could be persuaded to see the weakness of the case against Reyos and the strength of his alibi. Frustratingly Governor Abbott still refuses to even consider looking into Reyos' case.

I contacted Reyos a number of times during the remainder of 2015 but received no replies. I knew he was free because he continued to send me news stories, but I had no idea how he was or what, if anything was happening in his case. In fact it was not until 2016 that I heard from him next and that was in response to another cause of great sadness for Reyos.

It was in November 2015 that Dennis Cadra died, although I only learnt of this sad news in January 2016. I contacted Reyos to offer my condolences, as I knew Reyos had come to regard him as a friend as well as a supporter. 'Yes, he was a remarkable man, a man of good character and great integrity. He'll definitely be missed in the legal profession.', Reyos wrote, before giving me an update on how he was. Little was happening in his case although he continued to contact people to promote the injustice.

I heard more from Reyos in 2016, and in April he told me he was 'doing fine'. He had been closely following the case of Jack McCullough, who had been convicted in 2012 of murdering Maria Ridulph in 1957. The police had found evidence that McCullough was at his home 40 miles from the scene of the murder, when the crime was committed, but this evidence was suppressed by the police and prosecutors in order to ensure a conviction in what was one of the country's coldest of murder cases. Soon after the murder McCullough underwent a polygraph test, which he passed. Thankfully despite the passage of more than half a century phone records still existed and these showed that McCullough was on the phone, at his home, just minutes before Maria was abducted.

McCullough had always maintained he was at home at the time, 40 miles away, and therefore could not have committed the murder.

The alibi issue in McCullough's case reminded Reyos of his own case. He wrote to me in April 2016:

> 'There are so many cases of wrongful conviction coming to light lately here in the U.S. Many are overturned via DNA. I just wish that there was still available DNA in my case. It's a gross miscarriage of justice that the Odessa Police Dept. destroyed all the crime scene evidence.'

Thankfully McCullough had his conviction overturned and is now a free man. However, sadly, as with the murder of Father Patrick Ryan, the identity of Maria Ridulph's killer remains a mystery and he will almost certainly get away with murder, taking his secret to the grave.

If it were possible to look at telephone records from December 1981 it may be possible to help shed some light on who was responsible for Father Ryan's murder. After all, Father Ryan was at his home but suddenly rushed away, leaving food on the stove. It seems likely he would have received a phone call, which was responsible for him leaving his home very quickly. Phone records would show where that call was made from, which could be relevant.

Although the police in Odessa destroyed evidence in Reyos' case it has never been clear whether police in Denver City did so too. Although the Odessa police would have held the key evidence, Denver City would have also had records of enquiries they made, particularly before the Odessa Police became involved in what had previously been believed to be a missing person's case. Father Ryan's phone records would surely have been checked. If the Denver City police were willing to share any information they had then new light could be cast on this murder.

Very little happened in 2016 as we continued to try and promote the case. Reyos often told me he was 'doing fine', sometimes 'fine and well', keeping positive. By the end of the year he was adapting well to life and was enjoying the festive season.

The year 2017 began slowly and to increase momentum I decided to ensure this book was completed by the end of the year, to coincide with the 36th anniversary of Father Ryan's brutal murder. I had hoped to have it released in December 2016 but for personal reasons this had not been possible. Reyos was optimistic that the book would 'generate some attention whereby I will get some justice, after all these years.'

In September 2017 he told me very little was happening in his case and that he was now feeling the effects of his age, being 61 years old. Thankfully he is still in good health. Even with limited movements he has a degree of freedom, being free from prison, and is much more fortunate than those who are wrongly convicted and have to spend the remainder of their lives behind bars, suffering old age and infirmity whilst being punished in a hostile environment for a crime they did not commit.

Reyos added that he still hoped and believed that he would be exonerated, even if it looked less likely to happen than it had ten years earlier. 'I am still hopeful that justice will prevail someday. I've never lost hope.', he told me.

During September we learnt of the death of another of Reyos' strong advocates: former State Representative Paul Moreno, who sadly passed away at the age of 86. Moreno had been one of Reyos' strongest supporters at the time when it looked most likely that his case would be reviewed by the Board of Pardons and Paroles. Moreno had given so much hope which had helped Reyos remain strong. His death was indeed a very sad loss.

Despite the knock backs, Reyos remains certain that he will experience true freedom once again. 'Justice will prevail soon', he wrote to me on November 3, 2017. As this book goes to press he is, of course, still fighting to clear his name.

I asked Reyos what his hopes are for the future. He told me:

> 'For the future, continue to work on my wrongful conviction case. Help others who are in the same situation (in prison and innocent). After I am pardoned, return to my family in New Mexico. Perhaps go on a short vacation; visit Great Britain. Become like a motivational speaker, telling people about adversities and how to get through them (just like I did). I still have not lost hope that one day I WILL be exonerated. And pardoned.'

Fundamentally it is a simple life that Reyos desires. A life that that majority of us take for granted. He wants the ability to see his family, go to the cold mountains he loves so much, go out for a walk in a park at the weekend, and to enjoy a public holiday. All he wants is freedom of movement, which is a basic human right. It is, however, a human right which Reyos is deprived of because of the failings of the criminal justice system. He wants the criminal justice system to acknowledge it made an error and that he is not a killer. Whilst Reyos spent many years in prison, and continues to be confined to his small room during the evenings, weekends, and public holidays, Father Ryan's killer almost certainly continues to enjoy his life.

Importantly, Father Ryan's killer also remained free to commit further crimes. It is very possible, as the reader will soon discover, that Father Ryan's killer was responsible for another crime, a crime which Reyos could not have committed because he was 600 miles away at the county mental health facility in Albuquerque.

A Second Victim?

The following text is taken from the *Southern Cross*, the Roman Catholic diocesan newspaper for San Diego, dated November 1982. It is reproduced here to provide background information for the chapters which follow:

'Absolom, Absolum, My Son

Last week a man died. He did not die peacefully, although he was a man of peace. He did not die as good people should die, surrounded by love and loved ones. He did not die among friends although he had always surrounded himself with friends.

There was no one to pray with him and for him as he died, although he was a priest. He died many miles from home, murdered and left like something of no worth, although he was a man who valued each person for himself and would give them no less than the value he knew they owned in God's sight.

He was a fool for Christ; a man who accepted and trusted where we, who are more prudent and wise in the ways of the world, would not. He would turn no one from his door or his table. He would judge no man. He was killed wantonly by people who themselves with recipients of his charity, in the senseless violence so characteristic of this age and society. But, of all of us, he was most prepared for death, because all of his adult life he had lived on borrowed time. His health had been so precarious the death was his familiar, always at his elbow, always in his thoughts, always qualifying his plans. He often joked that he had been blessed with ordination only because no one expected him to survive his first year of priesthood, and laughed, because after 23 years of ministry he was looking forward to celebrating his silver jubilee. We who loved him – and he was greatly loved – had hoped that when it came, death would be gentle and kind, taking him by the hand, like a friend. But Father Ben was not a cautious man. He took the scriptures very seriously. He took his calling very seriously, and so he lived dangerously, risking himself not wisely, not sensibly, but in the only way he could. And in his imprudence, his foolishness, he shamed us in our comfortable self-protection.

So now we are left to mourn his passing, and experience again the universal wounding that is infected whenever evil works its destruction on the innocent and the good. But if we are to mourn him, let it be in a fitting way. Let us mourn him in sadness, not anger, for all that is not good in our world, and in love for what is.

Father Ben was not blind to the risk inherent in the way he lived, but he accepted it because he could see no other way to follow the Gospel warning, "Whatsoever you do to the least of these, you do to me," and in his relentless search for God, he took all who came his way into himself, and gave what he had without reserve.

In his physical frailty and stubborn commitment he was completely vulnerable and well aware of it. But the image of the crucified Christ, in all of his utterly defenseless love and self-giving, was always before his eyes and bound him in ways we cautious ones could not fully understand.

So, if we are to mourn him, let it be in a fitting way. Let it be in a way that will draw us to greater vulnerability and less-protectiveness, let it be with understanding, or at least an effort towards it, of the tormented creatures whose injured morality gives no value to human life and no respect to goodness.

If we are to mourn Father Ben, let us do it in a way he would value, taking on ourselves something of the burden he carried: that of bringing the presence of Christ to those who do not know him and risking their rejection and abuse.

It is a heavy burden, and few of us could heft it with the same dogged self-immolation that he did. But we can all give a little more of ourselves, drop a few more defenses, mortgage a little more comfort and safety, to carry Christ mission into the dangers zones of unbelief.

If we are not brave enough to take up the challenge of martyrdom, of standing up for Christ in the marketplaces of our lives, perhaps we can draw strength from this small man, so weak in body and so invincible in faith and achieve with him, in faith, what we cannot do alone.

It would be a fitting way to mourn a man of God and something of value to offer in exchange for a life so freely given.'

Father Ben

Father Benjamin Carrier

Father Ben was the name by which Father Benjamin Carrier was best known by his congregation. Although commonly known as Father Ben, I shall call him Father Carrier.

It was around 2pm on Wednesday November 10, 1982, and a cleaning maid was carrying out her duties at the El Rancho Motel, 2201 S. 4th Avenue, Yuma, Arizona.

Entering room 32, using the motel's master key, she saw, in one of the two beds, the figure of a small man covered with a blanket up to his shoulders. He was facing downwards, his face in his pillow.

The room should have been vacated by noon, so it was a little unusual for someone to still be present, but at first the maid assumed the man must be ill, perhaps hung-over, and had overslept.

However, when he failed to respond to any of the maid's calls, and was seen to be completely still, the maid hurried away, realizing there was something seriously wrong and fearing the worst, and reported the matter to the manager.

The manager went to look and was quickly sure the man was dead. This was not, however, a case of a natural death. The man had both his hands and feet securely bound with black electrical tape. It appeared to be a murder and the police were called.

Detectives Richard Stallworth and Brian Rodgers were assigned the case. There was no wallet on the man's person or in the room. It seemed likely it had been taken by his killer or killers.

There was no ID for the man, with any such cards or papers having probably been in his wallet. When he had checked into the motel, at around 3pm the previous day, he had identified himself as a priest and, presumably, gave his real name. Father Carrier, aged 54, was the parish priest for the Our Lady of Light church in Descanso, 130 miles away in the state of California.

The victim was wearing trousers and there was no evidence of sexual assault. A medical examination showed he had died of asphyxiation. A broken Rosary was found in one of his trouser pockets. Might it be possible the Rosary was used to help strangle the unfortunate man?

The victim was just over 5 foot tall, and weighed less than 100 pounds. It would later transpire he had suffered serious ill health for almost all his life, resulting in him being very frail. It would have been a simple task to overpower him. Binding his hands and legs, and then killing him, seemed somewhat unnecessary for a simple robbery, especially when strangulation can take several minutes when there are far quicker and easier methods of murder.

Had theft of a wallet and pick-up truck been a motive this could have been carried out without resorting to any great violence, let alone murder. And why kill for a pick-up truck if it is then abandoned soon after? There had to be more than robbery for this crime, but the police and those who knew the victim feel certain that was the motivation for this terrible crime.

I should make it absolutely clear at this point that there is no evidence to suggest Father Carrier carried out the seedy activities undertaken by Father Ryan. There is no evidence of any homosexual tendencies and his reasons for traveling to Yuma and staying at the motel are unknown. There is also no known connection between Father Carrier and the Jemez Springs complex. However, I think there is reason to suspect that Father Ryan and Father Carrier were killed by the same man; a man with a criminal dislike towards members of the priesthood.

The deceased was last seen at around 5pm the previous day, beside the motel's swimming pool. It was unclear when the crime had been committed. Reyos could not have committed this murder because he spent all of November 9 heavily drinking before being taken to the county mental health facility in Albuquerque, 600 miles from Yuma.

The police quickly announced they had a description of the man they believed to be the killer. This man had been with Father Carrier at the motel. Whilst Father Carrier checked in, and paid for two men, the suspect was in Father Carrier's vehicle.

The priest's companion was described as being tall, sullen-faced, with long blond hair. He was believed to be in his thirties or early forties. More recently the police have claimed this man was aged 20 to 25 years old and had light facial hair.

In fact the man had been seen by a number of individuals and had actually stayed with Father Carrier back in the parish. The suspected killer and another man had been seen leaving Yuma, in Father Carrier's company, on Monday November 8. They had left Yuma at 9:30pm that Monday, with parishioners believing Father Carrier had a meeting in El Centro. Father Carrier had only met the two men earlier that day, and it is unknown if they had ever encountered each other at any earlier time.

The three men did indeed travel to El Centro, in Father Carrier's pick-up truck, driven by the priest. They spent the night there, before heading to Alpine the following morning.

A friend of Father Carrier's, by the name of Father Alan Beauregard, was sat in Nino's restaurant in Alpine at 8am on the Tuesday morning when Father Carrier and the two men walked in. It was a chance encounter, although Carrier visited the area every couple of months or so and the two priests would often meet during those visits.

The three men sat with Father Beauregard, who later gave descriptions of Father Carrier's companions. One of the men was described as being French-Canadian, with a Canadian accent. This man was very talkative. He had dark, curly hair. The other man had a sullen appearance and what were described as "angry eyes". He had long blond hair. This man barely spoke.

Another witness described the men, one of whom appeared to be in his early 30s and was Canadian. The other man was thought to be around ten years older and was from Oklahoma.

In November 2016 a news article on the KYMA news website described the two men as being white men, aged in their 20s to early 30s, both about 5 feet 6 inches in height and of average build. One may have light facial hair and one with medium length, brown hair and light skin. One of the suspects is noted as having a tattoo on the under side of his left forearm. The article also revealed that one of the suspects with a cane decorated with a skull on the top and a slight Southern accent. These descriptions are at odds with the details released in 1982.

The original descriptions are consistent with descriptions given by people who briefly saw the men at the rectory back in Yuma.

Carrier told Father Beauregard that they had spent the previous night in El Centro and that they had now come to Alpine. The purpose of the trip, Father Carrier further told, was that the blond man was suffering from a serious lesion on his foot. In Alpine a friend of Father Carrier's, Dr Petersen, would treat the lesion. Dr Petersen often helped treat those who Father Carrier brought to him.

After being treated the three men were to head to Yuma. It seems very likely that Father Carrier was genuinely trying to help the men.

As in Father Ryan's case, Father Carrier's 1981 Toyota pickup truck had been taken from the parking lot. It was found in the early hours of Saturday November 13 in a street in Las Vegas and was impounded for forensic examination. Hundreds of fingerprints were lifted from the truck, and the crime scene, but they did not match any suspect. Many potential suspects were identified, and some arrests were made, but there was no evidence linking those suspects to the murder.

The police felt sure that the killer was the blond man who had taken advantage of Father Carrier's generous and caring attitude and had bound him up before robbing and killing him. Although he was not with Father Carrier when the two men checked into the motel, the French-Canadian may also have been involved. Neither man was ever identified.

During Father Carrier's time at the parish, the rectory at Riverside Drive, Descanso became somewhat notorious for the types of people who sought sanctuary there. People often arrived looking for somewhere to stay, and would be there for any period of time from a night to several weeks, or even months.

These people included those down on their luck, who needed temporary help, as well as hitchhikers who Father Carrier had offered a bed for a night before they continued their journey. Whilst many were considered to be harmless, parishioners were concerned by the drug users, ex addicts, alcoholics, felons who were on parole and released prisoners who, for a while, considered the rectory to be their home. Many were picked up by him, others brought by the police, others heard about his generosity and arrived knowing he would offer them a place to stay. It was well known throughout California and, it is believed, even further afield, that Father Carrier would offer a bed to anyone who needed help.

Father Carrier did not share their concerns, believing it to be his Christian duty to care for those who needed help. They were his "Lost Children", he would often say.

'He was notorious for indiscriminately picking up hitchhikers, however dubious or undesirable their appearance or the circumstances.', according to Enid Lanyon, author of the book

'Simply Benjamin' (a comprehensive and well-researched biography of Father Carrier).

His generosity had been abused on many occasions. Often he found belongings to have been stolen. Once the Sunday collection from Mass was stolen. Once he was tied up and robbed at knifepoint by those who he had taken in and tried to help.

On another occasion he was betrayed by a couple who hailed from Las Vegas. Charlie had been a drug dealer, who was married to a belly dancer named Gypsy. Charlie, it was claimed, was clean of drugs and was a reformed character. Father Carrier trusted the couple and one day allowed them, accompanied by three others who were staying at the Rectory, to take his car for a trip to the beach. He also gave them his credit card so that they could buy gas. They returned and all seemed fine. Two days later Charlie left the rectory and Gypsy was to follow. Father Carrier later learnt, from his credit card company, that his card had been used for a large purchase, amounting to several hundred dollars. By this time Gypsy had left, leaving a letter telling Father Carrier that money had been stolen to buy drugs. Although furious with the pair, the kindly priest later resumed contact with them but never received any of his money back.

Could there be some connection with the drug dealer from Las Vegas and the fact his pick-up truck was found abandoned in Las Vegas after the murder? It is possible, but could be a coincidence.

However, these incidents did not stop him from carrying out what he believed to be the Lord's important work. "As long as I have even an empty bath for someone to sleep in, I'll not turn anyone away who comes to my door.", he is recorded as once telling one of his parishioners.

Although he was much respected in his parish, Father Carrier had a large number of people who were angered by those he brought into the rectory. He was 'trusting to the point of foolhardiness', some had believed. In fact just four weeks before his death some of his parishioners held a ballot to decide whether Father Carrier should leave the parish, on account of him hosting people considered to be undesirable.

Eventually the ballot showed the majority wanted him to stay but as a result of the doubt expressed by some, Father Carrier did briefly leave before the votes were counted.

The doubt expressed by a sizeable proportion of his parishioners may have contributed towards his state of anxiety in his final months. He was seen to be very troubled about something and somewhat depressed. His health had always been a concern but there was certainly something which particularly clouded his state of mind in the months leading up to that November encounter with his murderer.

Anxiety was not something he experienced only towards the end of his life, however. Even some of those who knew him reasonably well believe he had some sort of secret and was not being who he wanted to be. Indeed in his journal a few years before his death he once wrote (in French to make his words even more cryptic), 'My face is covered with a mask of joy. ... O, yes, a mask of apparent goodness, apparent sanctity!!! I always have an answer to everything that comes up. I am afraid to be Ben as Ben is.'

Who did Father Carrier want to be? What was he alluding to? Could it have any bearing on his murder, or was he simply killed because he was a kind man who was considered an easy target?

There is a similarity to the murder of Father Patrick Ryan, who was found in a motel room, laying face down with his hands bound behind his back, less than a year earlier. In both cases the killer had taken the victim's wallet and driven away in the victim's vehicle, before abandoning it. However, Father Carrier died of asphyxiation, whilst Father Ryan was bludgeoned to death.

Although the method of murder was different, the other aspects of the two cases are eerily similar and raise understandable questions as to whether the crimes were committed by the same man. If they were then it would be proof that James Harry Reyos is an innocent man, because he was at the county mental health facility on the day that Father Carrier was killed. Father Carrier's murder remains unsolved.

Who were 'the tormented creatures whose injured morality gives no value to human life and no respect to goodness' referred to in the article regarding Father Carrier's death? Who could have committed yet another wicked crime? And yet again, why was this crime committed?

Back in 1982 Detective Richard Stallworth told the Southern Cross, "I think we are dealing with the most amateur of suspects, a couple of guys hitching around the country who were half demented."

The question is had these half demented men who traveled around the country (or at least one of them), managed to travel to Odessa the previous year and had they committed another murder there? And following Father Carrier's murder did one of them travel to Boise, Idaho? A mysterious suicide in December 1982 could be connected to this unsolved crime.

The Unknown Wanderer

A few weeks after the murder of Father Carrier, on December 4, 1982, a bizarre incident took place in Boise, Idaho. A stranger, aged between 35 and 45, walked in to the Sacred Heart Church seeking confession. He was deeply tanned, with hair that had been bleached by the sun, but was colored brown at the roots. He was 6 foot tall, of athletic build and weighed 180 lbs. He was wearing western style clothing.

Although he sought to make confession he did not have the patience to wait, and whilst the priest performed this sacrament to another person, at some stage that afternoon the unknown man slipped a cyanide tablet into his mouth and would have died just seconds later. When precisely he swallowed the tablet is unknown, and he may have spent some time in the church before ending his life. All we know is that his body was discovered, lying under a pew, during the late afternoon. Shortly before 5:45pm those arriving for the 6pm Mass noticed the body. A nurse, among the arriving congregants, checked for a pulse and confirmed the man was dead.

Sergeant Frank Richardson arrived and looked in the man's pockets, hoping to find some identification. A wallet in one of the man's pockets contained no form of identification. In another of the man's pocket was a typewritten note, interpreted as a cryptic suicide note, signed with the false name 'Wm. L. Toomey.'

The note read:

> 'In the event of my death, the enclosed currency should give more than adequate compensation for my funeral or disposal (preferred to be cremated) expenditures. What is left over, please take this as a contribution to this church. God will see to your honesty in this.'

The opening words of the letter imply that although he was prepared to commit suicide, he was not completely intent upon killing himself. Perhaps, had he been able to give confession, he would not have died. Alternatively he may have taken a low does of cyanide and, naively, was not certain it would result in his death and believed medical assistance could potentially save his life.

The name Wm L. Toomey is known to be false because the man clearly was not used to signing that name. The signature looked very hesitantly written and unnatural in the opinion of experts. Everyone with the name William Toomey was traced, with no missing persons of that name. Wm L. Toomey is the name of a Boston based company which manufactures garments for priests and nuns. Campaigners for Reyos believe the mystery man was, or had been, a priest himself because it was otherwise a very unusual choice of pseudonym. Enquiries found no connection between this company and the dead man.

Interestingly $1900 in cash was found in his pocket in $100 bills, which, the note explained, was to cover the costs of his funeral with any excess money being donated to the church. One of the bills had the telephone #224-4895 written on it. Two keys for a safety deposit box were also amongst the man's personal effects as was a key with the words 'Mills CTS, Lot #3' scratched on to it.

The man's identity remains a complete mystery, although it was determined his distinctive leather belt, which contained an unusual buckle bearing a Mexican 100 peso coin, was bought from a gift shop in Phoenix, Arizona. The man's fingerprints were run through the systems of both the Idaho police and the FBI. There was no match. He did not have any distinctive marks, tattoos or scars to help with comparisons with missing persons records. He had three teeth that had been filled (two upper and one lower).

It is believed the dead man was not local to Boise, and must have lived in one of the southern states, because he was deeply suntanned, with sun bleached hair, which would not be possible in Idaho in early December.

Frank Richardson, a detective in the Boise Police Department told journalists "He didn't want his name to be known, for whatever reason. It's strange."

The unidentified man was buried in a grey casket and 150 mourners attended his funeral, which was led by Reverend W Thomas Faucher, and which took place shortly after Christmas. The Reverend told the congregation that the Mass was for the dead man but also for all of those who had died in despair during the festive period, including three other people in the Boise area who had ended their own lives during the Christmas weekend. The request, to be cremated, could not be respected because the man's identity was unknown.

At the entrance to the Prayer Garden of the church there is a plaque bearing the names of those who have died and for whom prayers are dedicated. Unable to find the name of the individual, the church added the words 'Unknown Wanderer' to the plaque in order to commemorate the dead man. Some of the $1900 belonging to the 'wanderer', which was not needed for the costs of the funeral, were put towards the cost of the Prayer Garden.

Despite the mystery of the man's identity those who have studied the curious incident believe the man was responsible for killing priests, including Father Benjamin Carrier. The possible connection was first suggested by Boise Detective Frank Richardson, in 1993, whilst he was watching a documentary about Reyos' case. After watching the program, Richardson got in touch with Ryan's lawyer. Prior to Richardson making contact, Reyos had been completely unaware of the suspicious suicide.

Those who believe there is a connection have remarked upon the fact Father Carrier was murdered in early November, Reyos was charged a little over a week later, and then the man committed suicide in Boise three weeks after Reyos' arrest. It has been suggested the dead man felt guilt for both the murders of Father Ryan and Father Carrier (and possibly one other murder, as discussed later in this book) and felt even guiltier at seeing an innocent man accused of those murders. It is further argued that the belt buckle placed the Boise Doe in Arizona, the same state in which Father Carrier had been killed just weeks earlier. It is possible there is a connection but it is rather speculative.

Reyos certainly believes there is a connection, having told me:

> 'I still believe the Boise "John Doe" is linked to the crime. There has to be a way to identify him, especially now with the fingerprints and photo of him. Once his identity is known, the backtracking into his past can begin. "Who is he?", is the $64000 question.'

Indeed, who was the strange man who killed himself and what was the sin he wished to confess, the secret which he took to the grave? The truth is we will probably never know.

Reyos is angry that the police destroyed the forensic evidence for the murder of Father Ryan. Had that evidence been available it could have been compared with the fingerprints on record for the Boise Doe. It would have been possible to obtain DNA samples through exhuming the mystery man's remains and compared them with evidence found at the Sand and Sage Motel to suggest he may have been involved, or to completely eliminate him from the case. However, with the destruction of this evidence comparison is impossible. Reyos wrote to me about this in September 2017, to once again express his frustration at the police for destroying evidence:

> 'If ONLY the Odessa Police had not destroyed all the physical evidence from the motel room, I believe that the Boise John Doe's identity would've been ascertained. Had the DNA, all physical evidence from the motel room had been preserved, I would've been found INNOCENT.'

Certainly if the evidence had been kept the DNA of the killer would have been tested and compared with Reyos' DNA, which would clear Reyos of the murder. However, would it point to the Boise Doe as being that killer?

It is possible but the man may be entirely unconnected to the murders of Father Ryan, Father Carrier (and any other priest murders). The fact he does not match the description of the men seen with Father Carrier before his murder increases the unlikelihood that he was responsible for Father Carrier's murder. All we can say for certain is that he had a serious problem which led him to want to take his own life. We do not know that he committed any crime and the timing of the suicide, soon after the murder of Father Carrier, may have been entirely coincidental. He may have had a nervous breakdown, having struggled with a business or relationship. He may have wanted to clear his conscience for relatively minor sins before taking his life believing that it would help secure a place in Heaven. People commit suicide for all manner of reasons. Catholics believe that suicide is one of the greatest sins but he may not have been a practicing Catholic, instead being someone who had a faith and felt he had to take the final sacrament before killing himself.

It is possible that he was a killer but it is also very possible that the Boise Doe is unconnected, and is a red herring.

We cannot, therefore, say that the Boise Doe was responsible for either Father Ryan or Father Carrier's murders but given the mystery surrounding his identity it still needs to be looked into. If his identity can be determined then we can try and find out information about him and try and work out where he was, and what he was doing, on the dates on which the murders took place. We can then try and eliminate him from the murders or try and find information that might further connect him to the crimes.

With this in mind I spent many nights browsing the Internet in the hope of resolving the Boise Doe mystery. The internet has revolutionized the ability to obtain information that can be used to help solve mysteries. In 1983 when Reyos was convicted, of course there was no internet. His legal team and subsequently his campaigners were unable to find information that is now accessible at the click of a few buttons and perseverance.

I searched for people who had gone missing in 1982 and scrolled through the many individuals, comparing their photographs with those of the single photograph I had of the Boise Doe which showed his head slightly turned as he lay dead on the church floor. I was not able, that day, to find any possible matches for men who went missing in 1982 and I began to wonder whether the dead man had been reported missing at all. Undeterred I began looking through those who had gone missing in 1981 and after approximately an hour a face jumped out at me.

I will not name the man, who had gone missing in June 1981. He was described as having sandy brown hair. Like the Doe. He was described as having grey hair around his temples. Like the Doe. The heights matched. The builds were similar. The missing man looked to me like he could have been the Doe.

I exclaimed in pleasure. Could I have solved a mystery that had been challenging the minds of so many from a time when I was only a matter of a few weeks old?

The missing man was recorded as being feared to have been killed. He had been traveling to Canada in his truck and was never seen again. A man was later seen trying to impersonate him and money was taken from his bank account. The truck was found a few months later abandoned.

Although the circumstances of the disappearance were not in line with what I would expect, the similarities in appearance, and the fact the man went missing just months before Father Ryan's murder and only the year before the bizarre suicide, had to be investigated further.

I contacted organizations in the USA to try and establish whether he could be the Doe. Key amongst these organizations is the Doe Network, a volunteer organization which I had once volunteered with. I was highly disappointed to receive no response from these organizations. In fact I have contacted the Doe Network several times about different cases and have never received a response. It appeared I was constantly working against a wall of silence. Those who claimed to work to find the missing and identify the nameless were failing in their mission and were not even trying to achieve their aims.

After many attempts at working with the amateur sleuths I decided to make contact with the professionals, and so I contacted the Boise Police Department, but heard nothing. I also contacted journalists I knew in both Texas and Idaho to try and put pressure on the police to look into the possibility that this man may have committed suicide at Boise. Eventually the police did look into the case and found that the man whose photograph I had seen was not the Boise Doe. Feeling deflated I realized the search had to continue.

It was in September 2017 that I next came across someone who I felt could have been the man who committed suicide in December 1982. The man, who again I will not name, went missing in March 1982. He was 41 years old, 5'7" tall, suntanned, with light hair that was grey at his temples. He was possibly suffering from depression at the time of his disappearance.

The man was from Florida, which is a very long way from Idaho, but there was such a strong resemblance between the two men that I really believed I had finally identified the Boise Doe.

I contacted Reyos the next day and eagerly awaited his response. I also contacted the Doe Network, again receiving no response. Finally, I heard from Reyos. He too saw a strong resemblance between the two men but Reyos had access to information which I did not. Looking at the autopsy records for the Boise Doe he was able to tell me that the dead man had brown colored eyes whereas the man who went missing in March 1982 had blue colored eyes.

Other than that they were virtually identical but they could not have been the same person.

Reyos has also spent much of his limited internet time searching for the man's identity and has found several people who look very much like the Doe, but upon further investigation it has been discovered that they could not be him.

Both Reyos and I will keep trying to find out the identity of the Boise Doe but it remains as much a mystery today as when he stepped foot in the Sacred Heart Church 35 years ago.

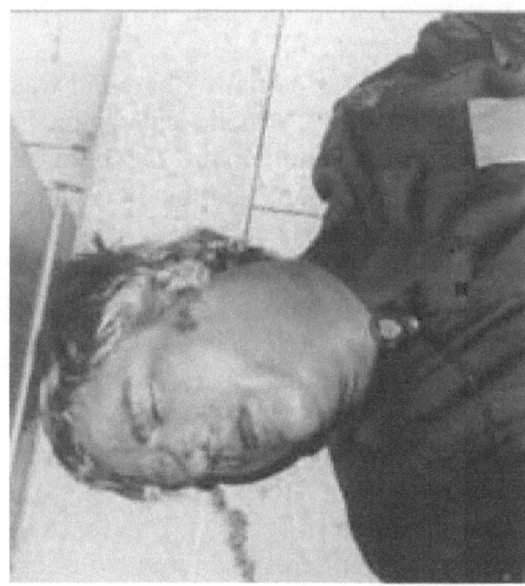

The man who committed suicide at the Sacred Heart church in Boise. Who is he? Could he be connected to the murders of Father Patrick Ryan and Father Benjamin Carrier?

Other Priest Murders

Father Ryan and Father Carrier were just two priests to be murdered in the USA in 1981 and 1982 and it has been suggested that both were victims of a serial killer.

Late one evening in August 1982 Father Patrick Gerard, a Roman Catholic priest who served at St Francis' Cathedral in Sante Fe, New Mexico, received a telephone call at his rectory. The caller identified himself as Michael Carmello and asked that a priest come quickly to a rest stop a short distance away near Waldo, a district of Santa Fe. He was asked to go there in order to give the Last Rites to his grandfather, who was dying of a heart attack.

The priest could not help because he was partially blind and was unable to drive in the dark. He asked that Carmello call again in fifteen minutes, presumably knowing that another priest would be present by that time. The telephone rang again quarter of an hour later and Father Reynaldo Rivera, pastor of the cathedral, answered and soon later left the rectory and drove away. He never returned.

It was two days later that Father Rivera's body was found. He had been tied up and shot in the stomach. His vehicle was nowhere to be seen, and was later found abandoned 110 miles away, just east of Grants, New Mexico, with an empty gas tank.

We can assume that it was the killer who made the telephone call because there was no man dying of a heart attack at the rest stop. Police also traced everyone with the name Michael Carmello, and ruled them out of the investigation. The murderer had lured the priest to that location in order to kill him. The motive is uncertain because Father Rivera had no valuables upon his person and the only things that appeared to have been taken were the materials he used to administer Last Rites. It appeared the killer was a man who hated the priesthood, committed the murder and (as with Father Ryan's murder) stole a trophy as a souvenir of the crime.

It has been suggested that Father Rivera was not specifically targeted because the caller could not have known which priest would answer the telephone. However, if he had done his research he would have known that one of the priests could not drive at night and that there was a good chance that Father Rivera would pick up the call.

The police believed more than one man had to be involved in order to overpower Father Rivera, although this is not necessarily the case because a man on his own could overpower another man, if he was armed with a gun. At gunpoint Father Rivera would probably have cooperated.

The police further believe the priest was taken by the killers, in their vehicle, and shot where his body was found. They then returned to steal Father Rivera's car.

No one has ever been arrested in connection with this murder. Reyos was, however, questioned about it whilst under arrest for the murder of Father Ryan, given that both men were priests.

Almost two years later, on July 20, 1984, Father John Kerrigan disappeared in Ronan, Montana, and has never been seen since. He had only been in Ronan for a few days, having been transferred from another parish. His bloodstained clothing was later found off a highway near Flathead Lake. A coat hanger was found nearby, covered in blood. It was thought the coat hanger, which was bent out of shape, had been used somehow in subduing Father Kerrigan. In a pocket of the bloodstained shirt was a $100 bill. A week later the police found his car abandoned, five miles from where the clothes were discovered. The car and its trunk were found to be covered in blood but the killer had taken steps to wipe away fingerprints. Robbery was seemingly not the motive because Father Kerrigan's wallet was found in the trunk, and was found to contain $1200 in cash.

Given the amount of blood in the vehicle it is assumed that Father Kerrigan was murdered. A shovel was found in the car, with blood on it. It is possible this was used to kill the priest, and may also have been used to help bury him. It appeared that his killer had a dislike for the priesthood, if not Father Kerrigan himself.

Interestingly a man named Curtis Holmen went missing from Missoula, Montana, two days after Father Kerrigan's disappearance. His body has never been found but his truck was found abandoned 40 miles from where Father Kerrigan's vehicle was found abandoned. One theory is that Holmen committed suicide but Holmen's brother believes he may have also been a victim of Father Kerrigan's murderer.

Both Father Rivera and Father Kerrigan were members of the Franciscan Order to priests. Both were killed in a way that resulted in a loss of large amounts of blood. Both had their vehicles stolen but theft was not the motive in either case. And in each case the killer wiped their fingerprints from the victim's vehicle. It seems likely that Fathers Rivera and Kerrigan were murdered by the same man or men.

Could these two murders be connected with those of Father Ryan and Father Carrier? The *modus operandi* used is very different but there is one possible connection: interestingly Father Kerrigan is known to have been a sex offender, who had stayed at the Jemez Springs Center for three months in 1983.

Could Father Kerrigan's killer have been a victim of abuse and sought revenge? Could he have also sought revenge on the other three priests murdered in 1981 and 1982? He may very well have been killed as a result of his sexual abuse, but I find it unlikely that there is any connection with the murders of Father Ryan and Father Carrier.

It seems likely to me that Fathers Ryan and Carrier were murdered by the same man or men, and that Fathers Rivera and Kerrigan were killed by an unrelated man or men. It does, however, demonstrate that there were multiple priests being murdered at around the same time as a result of their abuse. It is also of interest that Fathers Ryan, Carrier and Rivera were murdered in states that bordered one another, all within the same 12 month period. However, it is important to stress that there is no evidence that Father Carrier or Father Rivera were sex offenders.

Above (top): Father Rivera and (bottom): Father Kerrigan

The Real Killer?

If Reyos did not commit the murder of Father Patrick Ryan, then who did? In March 2012 I received an email from a person I will not name regarding a man who had been in some form of relationship with my correspondent's mother-in-law. I will refer to this man simply by the first name Drew. Drew came into the mother-in-law's life in 1992 but he used a false name. He claimed to be hiding from some dangerous individuals who had killed his father. Drew never had anything registered in his name and to all intents and purposes there was no record of his existence.

There is a reason why he lied about his true identity and that is because he was a fugitive from the police. In 1977 and 1981 he committed armed robberies. In 1981 he committed an armed robbery in Odessa and was imprisoned in Ector County, having been convicted and sentenced to 10 years imprisonment on August 14, 1981. However, he was released on an appeals bond shortly before the murder of Father Ryan and disappeared. He was, I was told, a very violent individual. 'He is a little psychotic and seems to have visions of how things took place that change depending on his audience.', one of the emails read. He also allegedly lied about how he received a gunshot wound, claiming he had been injured in Vietnam when in reality he was shot during an armed robbery.

Drew was 30 years of age in December 1981 at the time of Father Ryan's murder. He was approximately 6'1" or 6'2" in height; much taller than 5'4" Reyos who was alleged to have overpowered a significantly larger Father Ryan. He was, according to my correspondent, bisexual.

Interestingly he claimed to have had December 22 as his birthday even though it was not his birthday. Father Ryan was murdered late on the previous night but it is a rather curious lie to create.

Drew has, I am told, a fascination with Christianity and allegedly helped found a church. 'He has a preacher friend who is indicted in Cameron for cruelty to animals … He was so involved in starting this church and being an Elder of the church.'

I am always cautious about information I receive by email. I have been involved in dozens of cases in Britain and the USA and several of those cases have been very high profile. As I have said earlier there are people who have tried to discredit me and campaigns I have been involved in, in order to cause disruption that robs an innocent person of the chance of having their name cleared. Email offers a great opportunity for anonymity and so it is ideal for people who want to deceive. However, the correspondent who brought Drew to my attention had certainly used her real name and because she had used her work email address I was able to discover she had a respectable job and I could find out where she worked and, if need be, have people go to visit her for more information. This was not consistent with someone who was lying to me; a liar would have set up a free email account and not allowed me to so easily obtain her full name, work address and telephone number.

I sent the information to Jeff Blackburn who at the time I believed was still interested in Reyos' case. But short of more details and anything tangible to connect Drew with the murder what could I do? There were some grounds for further investigation but no actual evidence to persuade the police to look once again at a murder investigation which as far as they were concerned was closed.

However, there remains the strong possibility that my correspondent had a personal vendetta against Drew and wanted to cause difficulties in his life by trying to implicate him in a murder.

Even if Drew was responsible for the murder, which seemed possible but there was no actual evidence to suggest he could have been, it would require him to confess in order to be convicted. With no surviving forensic evidence and no eyewitnesses to the crime, and with the justice system believing it had the right man, there was no other way to implicate Drew, or anyone else for that matter, in the crime.

James Harry Reyos did not kill Father Ryan, so who is the real killer? What do we actually know? The answer is, unfortunately, very little,

We can be very sure that Father Ryan knew his killer, even if they had only recently met by the time of the attack. They must also have arranged to meet at the Sand and Sage Motel, perhaps organizing a rendezvous the day before Father Ryan's death.

Father Ryan had originally asked Reyos to go round to his home on the evening Monday December 21, 1981 (the day of the murder), to show Father Ryan his photograph album. This had been arranged the previous Friday. However, on Sunday December 20, 1981, according to Reyos, Father Ryan went round to Reyos' apartment and told Reyos that "tonight would be a good time to bring your photo album over because tomorrow night I will be busy."

Reyos believes the fact Father Ryan drove away from Charlie Bostick's house, leaving Reyos there, was further evidence that Father Ryan was in a hurry to get home in order to prepare to meet someone later that day. Reyos muses:

> 'Why would he just drive off leaving me at the bondman's house, if he had no plans? It would seem like he would have waited for me but, instead, he was in a hurry for some reason.'

Later that day, certainly, Father Ryan was at home. He was cooking food over a stove when something caused him to hurriedly leave, leaving the food on the stove. Did he receive a phone call from the person he was intending to meet, asking him to leave instantly? Something made him rush away, to the Sand and Sage Motel, where he met his killer. Or did someone come to his door and they drove to Odessa together?

The killer was large and strong, sufficiently so to overpower Father Ryan. He may have had an accomplice, if only to help move Father Ryan's vehicle, and travel away in his own vehicle. Certainly two vehicles were moved, one being abandoned in Hobbs. The killer, and any accomplice, presumably had a connection with Hobbs.

The killer must have been able to drive, but unfortunately we have no clues as to what type of vehicle he drove.

The crime itself was not well planned, and was perpetrated by someone who had minimal knowledge of forensics, because a large amount of forensic evidence was left behind. It was only because the police did not identify the killer as a suspect that he evaded capture. Had he been identified as a potential suspect there would have been an abundance of evidence to link him to the crime. Given the number of cigarette butts in the motel room, it is likely that the killer was a smoker.

The murder appeared to have been a rage killing, with far more violence and damage to the room than what was necessary. It was therefore likely that the killer had hatred towards Father Ryan personally, or to the priesthood. He may have been someone who had been abused by a priest. The killer would have had homosexual tendencies even if he did not identify as being a homosexual.

The killer would almost certainly have a long history of violent behavior, including criminal convictions for assault. He may then have gone on to kill Father Benjamin Carrier the following year.

Although Reyos meets some of the above criteria, he was 200 miles away. The alibi and forensic evidence show he was not responsible for the murder. Unfortunately a large number of men could meet the criteria above. We simply do not have sufficient information regarding the killer to be able to determine his identity. There are no witness descriptions of either him or his car. There is, of course, no forensic evidence.

Therefore we can only hope that one day the killer makes a confession, on his deathbed or in a drunken state, and that this information comes to our attention. Alternatively, if he had an accomplice, the accomplice could hopefully provide some information. The killer and any accomplice may have confided in someone. Or if anyone reading this book has suspicions that some one they know, or knew, could have been somehow involved in the murder then I would urge them to make contact.

It has now been 36 years since Father Ryan was brutally murdered, and it has been 35 years since Reyos was first sent to prison (to await trial) for the crime. It is a double tragedy of wasted lives and wasted years and we can only hope that some peace can be forthcoming for both Father Patrick Ryan and James Harry Reyos.

The final words of this sad tale must be with Reyos. In one of his many immaculately written letters he told me:

> 'I will NEVER give up trying to clear my name. As you know, there are many supporters backing me. We must all continue the fight, to see justice prevail. The fight for justice is not only for me, it's for Father Ryan too, to see that his killer is brought to justice.'

And just days before this book went for publication he told me:

> 'I am like David going up against Goliath. The state of Texas being Goliath, and me being David. I have a battle to be won!!!

Scott, it's been a battle!! However, I truly believe that I will win, in the end. I await for JUSTICE to prevail.'

www.ingramcontent.com/pod-product-compliance
Lightning Source LLC
Chambersburg PA
CBHW020421220526
45464CB00002B/518